W9-CPY-602

Contents

Contents

Introduction

I wrote this little book to help the American traveler with less than perfect mastery of the French language but who, nevertheless, is eager to interact in French while visiting France.

I found myself in exactly that situation many years ago when I first entered the United States. Having studied British English with great passion, but having had very little practice in oral communication, I was looking forward to honing in on those skills and finally practicing English in real-life situations. Surely among millions of friendly New Yorkers, there would be some who would enjoy speaking with me. Surprise: my host family was dumbfounded when they realized that my speaking skills did not by any stretch of the imagination match my writing skills.

A *Perfect Phrases in English* book would have been a treasure for me. Too late for me, but not for you!

In this book, I have included phrases to help you communicate with native French speakers throughout your trip, from basic courtesy-related phrases such as *Bonjour Monsieur,* which are so useful when setting the tone in any situation, to more situation-specific phrases designed to help you with essential needs such as asking for fresh towels in a hotel or ordering a drink at a café. The organization of phrases within the book is based on major themes such as Hotels, Money, Shopping, and Entertainment. The phrases are mostly those

I deemed essential and practical for getting around as a tourist and include survival phrases such as *Où est... ?* (Where is . . . ?) or *Ça fait combien... ?* (How much is . . . ?) However, I did include some conversational phrases for those of you who would like to forge relationships with native French speakers. The index provides additional help in looking up the phrase you need.

Each chapter includes several main entries covering a specific situation or need, such as *Est-ce qu'il y a une station de métro près de l'hôtel?* (Is there a subway station near the hotel?) In addition to an English translation, each entry provides a phonetic representation of the French pronunciation, designed to help you feel confident speaking French. Most of the phonetic representations are self-explanatory, but note that the transcriptions **ih**, **ah**, **oh**, and **uh** stand for the French nasal sounds represented by the letter combinations *in* (*im*), *an* (*am*), *on* (*om*), and *un* (*um*). Also note that a capital **U** in the transcription stands for the last sound you hear in the English words *few* or *pew*, and that **euh** stands for the vowel sound in an English word like *perk* or *murky*. Remember, however, that you don't have to pronounce perfectly to get your point across, and the French will appreciate your efforts to speak their language.

What I think you'll find unique and, I hope, enjoyable, is that each entry is accompanied by detailed explanations of the cultural context in which you might come across or use the phrases, enabling you to make the most of your encounters with French speakers during your trip. Each main entry is also followed by other phrases that reinforce or pertain to the main entry, which will greatly increase your ability to communicate.

I hope you will be able to use many of these phrases on your trip and wish you **bonne chance** and many happy memories!

Pronunciation Guide

In addition to an English translation, each entry provides a phonetic representation of the French pronunciation designed so that you will feel confident speaking French. Most of these phonetic representations are self-explanatory, but this guide will clarify elements of French pronunciation with which you might not be familiar.

Most consonants are pronounced similarly in French and English, although the French *r* is guttural (produced in the throat), not forward in the mouth as it is in English. Some other things to keep in mind about consonants in French:

- The letter *h* is always silent.
- Many consonants, for example, *s*, *t*, and *d*, are silent at the end of words, unless the following word begins with a vowel sound.
- The equivalent of the English *th* sound does not exist in French. Pronounce it simply as *t*.

However, the pronunciation of vowels and vowel-consonant combinations vary quite a bit from French to English. In order to use the phonetic representations in this book to their full advantage, follow these guides for vowel sounds. (The letters in bold below are what you will see in the phonetic representations.)

- **a** is pronounced like the *a* sound in the word *father*.
- **ee** stands for many *i* or *y* sounds in French spelling; it is pronounced like the sound *ee* as in *heel*.
- **o** is pronounced like the sound *o* in *more* or *bored*.
- The vowel *e* is always silent at the end of a French word unless the *e* has an accent mark (*é*).

Some letter combinations containing the vowels *e* and *u* have unique sounds in French that do not exist in English. To get as close as possible to their authentic pronunciation, practice as follows:

- **euh** represents the sound of *u* in *lurk* or the sound of *e* in *perk* or the sound of *i* in *girl*. In French this sound is usually spelled: *e, eu,* or *œu*.
- Capital **U** represents the *final sound* in the English words *few* or *pew*. In French, it is normally spelled: *u*.

The phonetic representations **ah**, **ih**, **uh**, and **oh** stand for French nasal sounds where, in spelling, the vowel combines with *-n* or *-m* to produce a unique blended sound. The letter **h** after a vowel in the transcription reminds you that this vowel makes a special sound as described below:

- **ah** represents a nasal sound similar to the vowel sound in the word *pawn* or *lawn*. Be careful *not* to sound out the letter *n* or *m*; this is a vowel, not a consonant sound.
- **ih** represents a nasal sound similar to the vowel sound in *glance* or *chance*.

- **uh** represents a nasal sound similar to the *u* sound in *muddy*.
- **oh** represents a nasal sound similar to the *o* sound in *bonfire* or *conjugate*. Remember: *Do not* sound out the letters *n* or *m*.

Remember as you use this book, however, that you don't have to pronounce perfectly to get your point across and that the French will appreciate your efforts to speak their language.

Chapter 1

Good Manners

 Bonjour. *(boh-zhoor)*: Hello.

This is the basic everyday greeting used by anyone, young or old, in formal and informal settings. In a French-speaking country, it should always be followed by a title such as *monsieur, madame*, or *mademoiselle* when addressing adults who are not your friends. Be especially aware that French people who work in shops, stores, and other businesses expect customers to greet them as they enter their premises. Unlike American customers who are often very direct in stating what they want, French customers are expected to exhibit good manners and act politely toward the people who are there to assist them. This means saying *Bonjour, monsieur/madame/mademoiselle* before asking for service.

Never address the local baker or grocery clerk by his/her first name even if you see him/her regularly; first names are reserved for friends and relatives. In very formal settings such as government, corporate, or diplomatic circles, make the effort to learn appropriate titles such as *monsieur le directeur* (meuh-syeuh leuh dee-rek-teuhr), *madame la directrice* (ma-dam la dee-rek-trees), *monsieur le consul* (meuh-syeuh

1

leuh koh-sUl), or *madame le maire* (ma-dam leuh mer). This will be very much appreciated. If you know the last name of a person, you may use it and, for example, say *Bonjour, Monsieur/Madame Lafitte.* However this is not necessary; a simple *Bonjour, monsieur/madame* is quite acceptable.

Bonjour, monsieur.	Hello (to a man).
boh-zhoor meuh-syeuh	
Bonjour, madame.	Hello (to a woman).
boh-zhoor ma-dam	
Bonjour, mademoiselle.	Hello (to a young woman or a girl).
boh-zhoor mad-mwa-zel	

 Enchanté(e). *(ah-shah-tay):* Pleased to meet you.

This phrase, more frequently used by men than by women, is particularly delightful when used with appreciative people. Charm a lady by greeting her with this single lovely word which literally means "enchanted" or "charmed." To further impress your new acquaintance, you may use the entire phrase *Enchanté(e) de faire votre connaissance.* This phrase is often used by gentlemen greeting ladies in conjunction with a *baise-main* (bez-mih), a light kiss on the hand. A little less flashy or bewitching, but nevertheless pleasing, is the phrase *Heureux/Heureuse de faire votre connaissance.*

Enchanté(e) de faire votre connaissance.	Delighted to make your acquaintance.
ah-shah-tay deuh fer vot ko-nes-sahs	

Heureux/Heureuse de faire votre connaissance.	Happy to make your acquaintance.
euh-reuh/euh-reuhz deuh fer vot ko-nes-sahs	

 Comment allez-vous? *(ko-mah ta-lay voo):* How are you?

This classic phrase frequently accompanies a greeting and can be safely used with any adult. The *Bonjour. Comment allez-vous?* question can be answered with *Bien, merci. Et vous?* (byeh mer-see ay voo) (Fine, thank you. And you?) or *Pas mal* (pa mal) (Not bad) or *Comme ci, comme ça* (kom see kom sa) (So-so).

In informal settings or with children and young people, you may use the phrase *Comment ça va?* Your respondent will answer with *Bien* (byeh) (Fine). You may also abbreviate your question to *Ça va?*, making sure to raise the pitch of your voice on the second syllable. This can be answered with *Oui, ça va bien* (wee sa va byeh) (Yes, it's going fine) or *Non, ça ne va pas très bien.* (noh sa neuh va pa tray byeh) (No, it's not going so well.)

Comment ça va?	How are you? How is everything?
ko-mah sa va	
Ça va?	Are you doing OK?
sa va	
Ça va bien, merci.	I am fine, thank you.
sa va byeh mer-see	

Comment vous portez-vous? *(ko-mah voo por-tay voo):* How are you doing?

If you want to go beyond the casual salutation and ask how the person is doing, perhaps after an illness, ask: *Comment vous portez-vous en ce moment?* (How are you doing/feeling now?)

Mieux, merci.	Better, thank you.
myeuh mer-see	
Beaucoup mieux, merci.	Much better, thank you.
bo-koo myeuh mer-see	
Je me remets.	I am getting better.
zheuh meuh reuh-may	

 Je m'appelle... *(zheuh ma-pel):* My name is . . .

Introduce yourself socially by saying *Je m'appelle John.* This is different from filling in your last and first name under *Nom* and *Prénom* or your *Nom de jeune fille* (maiden name) on a questionnaire, a customs document, or any other official paper.

Mon nom de famille est Smith.	My family name is Smith.
moh noh deuh fa-mee ay smith	

 Je vous présente... *(zheuh voo pray-zaht):* This is . . .

Introduce your husband or wife by saying *Je vous présente mon mari/ ma femme* (zheuh voo pray-zaht moh ma-ree/ma fam). Introduce your friend or significant other by saying: *Je vous présente mon ami*

Marc/mon amie Martine. The French are generally more discreet—and they can also be more matter-of-fact—about relationships than are Americans. You may not find out until much later whether the word *ami* (male friend) or *amie* (female friend) was meant in the casual sense of "friend" or whether the person was a boyfriend or girlfriend. So be patient and listen for clues in the conversation! You may also introduce someone in a more casual way by saying: *Voici…* (This is . . .).

Je vous présente mon ami(e).	Let me introduce my friend.
zheuh voo pray-zaht mo na-mee	
Voici mon mari.	This is my husband.
vwa-see moh ma-ree	
Voici ma femme.	This is my wife.
vwa-see ma fam	

 Au revoir. *(o rvwar):* Good-bye.

This phrase is an appropriate way to say "good-bye" in any context, both in formal situations, as in *Au revoir, monsieur* (Good-bye, Sir) and informal situations, as in *Au revoir, Martine* (Good-bye, Martine). After six P.M. one says *Bonsoir* (literally, Good evening) instead of *Bonjour* (literally, Good day). However, while *Bonjour* is only used to say "Hello," *Bonsoir* is used for both "Hello" and "Good-bye."

Bonsoir.	Hello./Good-bye. (in the evening)
boh-swar	

Salut! *(sa-lU)*: Hi!/Bye!

Used in informal situations between good friends, relatives, and especially among young people, *Salut!* is the equivalent of "Hi!" as well as
"Bye!" When it is used to say "Bye," it is often followed by a phrase
such as *À bientôt* (See you soon), *À demain* (See you tomorrow), or *À
samedi* (See you Saturday).

À bientôt.	See you soon.
a byeh-to	
À demain.	See you tomorrow.
a deuh-mih	
À samedi.	See you Saturday.
a sam-dee	

 S'il vous plaît. *(seel voo play)*: Please.

S'il vous plaît is an amazingly versatile expression. *Un café, s'il vous plaît*
is simply "I'd like a cup of coffee, please." But the phrase is used much
more often than "please" in English. For example, you may use it to
get your waiter's attention: *Monsieur, s'il vous plaît!* is the equivalent of
saying "We need service here." In much the same way, it can be used
instead of *Excusez-moi* (eks-kU-say mwa) to approach a person when
you wish to ask for directions: *S'il vous plaît, Madame. Où se trouve la
Tour Eiffel?* (seel voo play ma-dam oo seuh troov la toor ay-fel) (Excuse
me, madam. Where is the Eiffel Tower?)

It is much better, however, to preface any kind of request for service or help with *Excusez-moi de vous déranger.* (eks-kU-say mwa deuh
voo day-rah-zhay) (Forgive me for disturbing you.) At first, this may

seem burdensome and excessive to an American, but it is absolutely the right thing to do to show your good manners to a French person, especially someone who may be rushed or preoccupied. By using this sentence, you acknowledge that you are intruding on someone's privacy.

In addition, *s'il vous plaît* can be used derisively or sarcastically. Consider the sentence: *Et elle descend toujours au Ritz, s'il vous plaît!* (And she always stays at the Ritz, if you please/no less!)

Un café, s'il vous plaît.	A coffee, please.
uh ka-fay seel voo play	
S'il vous plaît, Madame/ Monsieur/Mademoiselle.	Excuse me/Please, Madam/Sir/Miss.
seel voo play ma-dam/ meuh-syeuh/mad-mwa-zel	
Entrez, s'il vous plaît.	Please enter!
ah-tray seel voo play	
Par ici, s'il vous plaît.	This way, please.
par ee-see seel voo play	

 Merci. *(mer-see):* Thank you.

Bien, merci (Fine, thank you) is the perfect way to answer the question *Comment ça va?* Want to show a little more enthusiasm? Add: *Super! Merci mille fois!* (Super! A thousand thanks!) The basic thank you can be enhanced in a variety of ways: *Un grand merci* (uh grah mer-see) (A big thank you); *Merci beaucoup* (Thanks a lot); *Merci mille fois* (A thousand thanks), *Merci infiniment* (I am infinitely grateful).

Just like American children, French children are continually being reminded to say *Merci*, often in a typical reproachful way such as *Tu ne dis pas merci?* (tU neuh dee pa mer-see) (Don't you/we say thank you?) In contrast to American children, however, French children must also remember to add the appropriate title *monsieur/madame/mademoiselle* to their *merci* or they will embarrass their parents and be called *mal élevés* (mal ayl-vay), literally, "badly raised." To acknowledge someone's thanks, answer *De rien*, *Je vous en prie*, or *Il n'y a pas de quoi*. These phrases all mean "You're welcome./Don't mention it."

Bien, merci.	Fine, thank you.
byeh mer-see	
Super! Merci mille fois!	Great! A thousand thanks!
sU-per mer-see meel fwa	
Merci, Madame/Monsieur/ Mademoiselle.	Thank you, Madam/Sir/Miss.
mer-see ma-dam/meuh-syeuh/ mad-mwa-zel	
Merci beaucoup.	Thanks a lot.
mer-see bo-koo	
Merci mille fois.	A thousand thanks.
mer-see meel fwa	
Merci infiniment.	I am infinitely grateful.
mer-see ih-fee-nee-mah	
De rien.	You're welcome.
deuh ryeh	
Je vous en prie.	You're welcome.
zheuh voo zah pree	
Il n'y a pas de quoi.	Don't mention it.
eel nya pad kwa	

Être à la merci de... *(etr a la mer-see deuh):* To be at someone's mercy.

The phrase *Je suis à votre merci* (zheuh swee a vot mer-see) (I am at your mercy), can be said by a person who totally depends on another. If you want a really good place in a theater, you might want to appeal to the goodwill of the ticket booth clerk or other agent by saying: *J'aurais désiré une place au balcon, mais je suis à votre merci.* (zho-ray day-see-ray Un plas o bal-koh may zheuh swee a vot mer-see) (I would have liked a balcony seat, but I am at your mercy.)

 Excusez-moi. *(eks-kU-zay mwa):* I'm sorry./Excuse me.

Excusez-moi is another versatile phrase that can be used in many different contexts. Use it to say "I'm sorry" or "I apologize," for example, if you've accidentally bumped into someone. *Excusez-moi*, like *Pardon*, is an effective and polite way to begin your request. You may preface a request for directions by saying: *Pardon, Monsieur/Madame. Excusez-moi de vous déranger.* (Pardon me, Sir/Madam. Sorry to bother you.)

Having garnered the person's attention, you can then safely ask for directions: *Pourriez-vous m'indiquer la rue de la Madeleine?* (poo-ryay voo mih-dee-kay la rU deuh la ma-dlen) (Can you tell me where Madeleine Street is?)

Sometimes *Excusez-moi* is used to warn another person what you are about to do or say. You might use this phrase as you are about to squeeze through a crowded subway to reach the exit: *Excusez-moi. C'est mon arrêt!* (eks-kU-zay mwa say mo na-ray) (Excuse me. This is my stop!), or you might use the phrase as a lead-in to expressing your disagreement with someone: *Excusez-moi. J'ai quelque chose à vous dire.* (eks-kU-zay mwa zhay kel-keuh shoz a voo deer) (Excuse me. I have something to tell you.)

Excusez-moi, Madame/	Excuse me, Madam/Sir/Miss.
Monsieur/Mademoiselle.	
eks-kU-zay mwa ma-dam/	
meuh-syeuh/mad-mwa-zel	
Excusez-moi de vous déranger.	I'm sorry to bother you.
eks-kU-zay mwa deuh voo	
day-rah-zhay	
Excusez-moi de vous interrompre.	Forgive me for interrupting.
eks-kU-zay mwa deuh voo	
ih-tay-roh-pr	

Pardonnez-moi. *(par-don-nay mwa):* Pardon me.

Pardonnez-moi can be ambiguous. It is somewhat stronger than *Excusez-moi* as it implies begging forgiveness. You may use *Pardonnez-moi* or *Pardon* followed by the appropriate title *Monsieur/Madame/Mademoiselle* when you need a salesperson's or a waiter's attention or when you are about to ask someone to help you in any way: *Pardonnez-moi, Monsieur. Où sont les toilettes, s'il vous plaît?* (Pardon me, Sir. Where is the restroom, please?)

The French are well known for their tendency to disagree and play devil's advocate with one another. When they are about to disagree with someone, they will do it politely, but with a nuance of sarcasm, by saying something like: *Pardonnez-moi, mais je ne suis pas d'accord.* (Pardon me, but I do not agree.) In addition, the French tend to be cynical and direct about life's realities; don't be surprised to hear negative phrases such as: *Ça ne pardonne pas*, which is frequently used to say that there are severe consequences to certain actions: *L'amour ça ne pardonne pas.* (la-moor sa neuh par-don pa) (Love is not forgiving.)

Pardonnez-moi, Madame/ Monsieur/Mademoiselle.	Pardon me, Madam/Sir/Miss.
par-don-nay mwa ma-dam/ meuh-syeuh/mad-mwa-zel	
Pardonnez-moi, madame. Où sont les toilettes?	Pardon me, Madam. Where are the restrooms?
par-don-nay mwa ma-dam oo soh lay twa-let	
Pardonnez-moi, mais je ne suis pas d'accord.	Pardon me, but I disagree.
par-don-nay mwa may zheuh neuh swee pa da-kor	
Ça ne pardonne pas.	There's no excuse.
sa neuh par-don pa	

Chapter 2

Money Matters

 Pouvez-vous m'indiquer une banque? *(poo-vay voo mih-dee-kay Un bahk):* Can you direct me to a bank?

This phrase may be useful when you need access to an ATM. ATMs are located everywhere in French cities and towns, inside and outside banks and also mounted outside other commercial buildings. Be aware that French ATMs only accept a four-digit PIN, and there are no letters, only numbers, on the keypads. So at first you may wish to inquire inside a bank about the use of their ATMs. In addition, you can get information on the exchange rate *(le taux de change)* in the bank of the ATM you plan on using. French ATMs should allow you to select your language. Just look for the sign of the "hand" holding a card.

 Je cherche un bureau de change. *(zheuh shersh uh bU-ro deuh shahzh):* I am looking for a currency exchange.

You can exchange dollars for euros at your hotel or at any *banque*, *bureau de poste* (post office), or *grand magasin* (department store), as well as at the *aéroport* (airport), the *gare* (railway station), and at some *stations de métro* (subway stations). You will also find *les bureaux de change* (currency exchange offices) near popular tourist spots such as the Eiffel Tower in Paris.

In France *le taux de change* (currency exchange rate) is more or less spelled out at currency exchanges and banks. Note that it may differ from one location to another. Watch out for large price differences between the *prix d'achat* (purchase price) and the *prix de vente* (sales price) of a currency, as well as the price of any *commissions* (transaction fees). Those two factors can cause great disparities in the price of exchanging dollars for euros in different places.

Je voudrais changer 200 dollars en euros, s'il vous plaît.	I would like to exchange $200 into euros, please.
zheuh voo-dray shah-zhay deuh sah do-lar a neuh-ro seel voo play	
Quel est le taux de change du dollar à l'euro?	What is the exchange rate from the dollar to the euro?
kel ay leuh to deuh shahzh dU do-lar a leuh-ro	

 **Pouvez-vous me donner des billets de dix euros?** *(poo-vay voo meuh don-nay day bee-yay deuh dee zeuh-ro):* Can you give me some ten euro bills?

Since 1999, the French-speaking countries of Belgium, France, and Luxembourg, as well as many other European countries, have the *euro* as their common currency. The symbol € that represents the euro is a combination of the letter E (for Europe), the Greek letter *epsilon* (symbolizing European civilization), with two parallel lines crossing it (symbolizing the stability of the euro). In a price or other listing, placement of the euro sign varies. Since there are no official standards on placement, most countries have retained those of their former currencies. In France, an amount such as three euros fifty centimes can be written as *3,50€* or *3€50*. To indicate *centimes* (cents), sums are often expressed as decimals of the euro (for example, *0.05€* rather than *5c*). The most common abbreviation for cent is *c*, but it also may appear as *¢*.

J'ai besoin de monnaie.　　　　　I need change.
zhay beuh-zwih deuh mon-nay

 Où puis-je trouver un DAB? *oo pweezh troo-vay uh day-a-bay*
Where can I find an ATM?

Most banks in France have ATMs where *une carte de crédit* (credit card) or *une carte bancaire* (debit card) can be used for withdrawing cash. In addition, hotels, restaurants, shops, and supermarkets all accept credit cards. The most commonly accepted are MasterCard, EuroCard, Visa, American Express, and Diners Club.

An ATM is called *un DAB* (*un distributeur automatique de billets*) or *un point d'argent* and is probably the best way to withdraw cash while traveling in France, especially since the exchange rates at ATMs are usually the most favorable. Since some ATMs do not allow you to enter PINs longer than four digits, don't forget to change your PIN to a four-digit number at your home bank before traveling to France.

Voilà ma carte bancaire!　　　　There's/Here's my debit card!
vwa-la ma kart bah-ker

Acceptez-vous les chèques de voyage? *(ak-sep-tay voo lay shek deuh vwa-yazh):* Do you accept traveler's checks?

Although carrying credit cards may seem the most efficient and safest way to travel, American Express and other traveler's checks are still in use. Imagine being low on cash in a small French town around noon: the ATM network is down, the machine is out of cash, or it will not accept your PIN. Traveler's checks would certainly come in handy to pay for your lunch; later, you can use them when French shops reopen after the lunch break. Another advantage of traveler's checks is that, in case of theft or loss, unlike *l'argent liquide* or *les espèces* (cash) or credit cards, they can be replaced quickly at any representative office at no additional cost. Sign them once at the time of purchase and then a second time when you use each one, showing reliable identification such as your passport. *Les chèques de voyage* are accepted in stores, restaurants, hotels, and agencies almost everywhere. You can use them to pay for purchases and services, and you can also cash them.

Je vous paie avec un chèque de voyage.
zheuh voo pay a-vek uh shek deuh vwa-yazh

I'll pay you with a traveler's check.

Voilà mon passeport.
vwa-la moh pas-por

There/Here is my passport.

Chapter 3

Hotels

 Je voudrais une chambre simple. *(zheuh voo-dray Un shah-br sih-pl):* I would like a single room.

When you travel alone, ask for a single room with this simple phrase: *Je voudrais une chambre simple* (zheuh voo-dray Un shah-br sih-pl). Know that in old-fashioned French hotels, especially in Paris, a single room, although possibly quite charming, may be hardly big enough to fit a bed and a nightstand. If you stay in a small hotel, many of the rooms may be close to the street and therefore noisy. You may prefer a quieter room, in which case you will say: *Je voudrais une chambre tranquille.* (zheuh voo-dray Un shah-br trah-keel) (I would like a quiet room.)

Je voudrais une chambre simple.	I would like a single room.
zheuh voo-dray Un shah-br sih-pl	
Je voudrais une chambre double.	I would like a double room.
zheuh voo-dray Un shah-br doo-bl	
Je voudrais une chambre tranquille.	I would like a quiet room.
zheuh voo-dray Un shah-br trah-keel	

Je voudrais une vue.   I would like a view.

zheuh voo-dray Un vU

Je voudrais un lit de bébé.   I would like a crib.

zheuh voo-dray uh lee deuh bay-bay

 Est-ce qu'il y a une salle de bains privée? *(es keel ya Un sal deuh bih pree-vay):* Is there a private bathroom?

Hotels in Europe can still be small, family-run businesses. There is a great variety in price and comfort level, from simple one-star hotels to very expensive and luxurious five-star hotels. A one-star hotel may not have *un ascenseur* (an elevator) and the rooms may not have *une télé* (a TV). The French do not classify beds according to size (king, queen, double, or single). They will generally refer to *un grand lit* or *un petit lit* (big or small bed). If you want to be certain that your *chambre* (room) comes with a bathroom, be sure to remember this important phrase: *Est-ce qu'il y a une salle de bains privée?* It is advisable to ask if the bathroom is *en suite* (inside your room). *Une salle de bains* usually has a bathtub with a small handheld shower attachment (*la douche*) or *une douche* (shower) with no tub.

    If you're looking for the restroom in a public place such as a store or restaurant, don't ask for *une salle de bains*. That would definitely bring a smirk to your respondent's face; instead ask for *les toilettes* (lay twa-let) (the restroom).

Est-ce qu'il y a une salle de   Is there a private bathroom?

    bains privée?

es keel ya Un sal deuh bih pree-vay

Est-ce qu'il y a un ascenseur?   Is there an elevator?

es keel ya euh na-sah-seuhr

Est-ce qu'il y a une télé?   Is there a TV?

es keel ya Un tay-lay

Est-ce qu'il y a un grand lit?   Is there a big bed?

es keel ya uh grah lee

 Le petit déjeuner est compris ou à part? *(leuh peuh-tee day-jeuh-nay ay koh-pree oo a par):* Is breakfast included or separate?

Breakfast is often included in the price of the room in Europe, but is not guaranteed in France. Make sure to ask. A continental breakfast is customary and may include *une baguette*, *des petits pains* (rolls), *des croissants,* and sometimes *des pains au chocolat* (chocolate croissants). The breads are usually accompanied by *de la confiture* (jam) and *du beurre* (butter).

Les repas sont compris?   Are meals included?

lay reuh-pa soh koh-pree

Le parking est compris?   Is parking included?

leuh par-keeng ay koh-pree

Tout est compris dans le prix?   Is everything included in the price?

too tay koh-pree dah leuh pree

 Le WC est bouché. *(leuh vay-say ay boo-shay):* The toilet is clogged.

When you take possession of your hotel room, check it thoroughly, and report any problems to the manager. Check the plumbing. If a toilet or a sink is clogged, report the problem immediately. If you do not understand how to use the shower, ask someone to demonstrate its operation to you. European-style bathrooms often feature a bathtub or shower stall with a handheld shower apparatus. The operation of the shower or bathtub may not be obvious to you, and you want to be safe.

L'évier est bouché.	The kitchen sink is clogged.
lay-vyay ay boo-shay	
Le lavabo est bouché.	The bathroom sink is clogged.
leuh la-va-bo ay boo-shay	
Le robinet a une fuite.	The faucet has a leak.
leuh ro-bee-nay a Un fweet	
Je ne sais pas comment fonctionne	I don't know how the shower works.
la douche.	
zheuh neuh say pa ko-mah fohk-syon	
la doosh	

 La chambre n'a pas été nettoyée. *(la shah-br na pa zay-tay net-twa-yay):* The room has not been cleaned.

If you find your room not cleaned to your satisfaction, report: *La chambre n'a pas été nettoyée.* (The room has not been cleaned.) If there is no electricity, report: *L'électricité ne marche pas.* (The electricity is not working.)/*Il n'y a pas de courant.* (There is no power.)

L'électricité ne marche pas.	The electricity does not work.
lay-lek-tree-see-tay neuh marsh pa	
La télé ne marche pas.	The TV does not work.
la tay-lay neuh marsh pa	

Il n'y a pas de courant.   There is no power.
eel nya pa deuh koo-rah

Il n'y a pas assez de serviettes.   There are not enough towels.
eel nya pa za-say deuh ser-vyet

 Peut-on régler la climatisation? *(peuh-toh ray-glay la klee-ma-tee-za-syoh):* Can the air conditioning be adjusted?

Old-fashioned French hotels may not be air-conditioned or the temperature may be set too high for you. If you find it too warm, tell the receptionist it is too hot in the room, and ask if the air conditioning can be adjusted. If there is no air conditioning, a possible solution may be to *changer de chambre* (move to another room) with a different exposure. When staying in a big city such as Paris, the location of your room might contribute not only to the temperature but also to the level of noise you are exposed to. Another precaution to take when reserving a room is to be very clear about requesting *une chambre non fumeur* (Un shah-br noh fU-meuhr) (a non-smoking room) or *une chambre fumeur* (a smoking room) (Un shah-br fU-meuhr).

Il fait trop chaud dans la chambre.   It is too hot in the room.
eel fay tro sho dah la shah-br

Il y a trop de bruit.   There is too much noise.
eel ya tro deuh brwee

On a fumé dans cette chambre.   Someone smoked in that room.
oh na fU-may dah set shah-br

L'auberge de jeunesse est à côté de la mairie. *(lo-berzh deuh zheuh-nes ay ta ko-tay deuh la may-ree):* The youth hostel is next to the city hall.

For intrepid young travelers trekking through Europe, staying in *les auberges de jeunesse* (youth hostels) is still a money-saving and socially friendly choice. The *FUAJ* (*Fédération Unie des Auberges de Jeunesse*) is a nonprofit organization founded in 1956. You can make a reservation online or by fax, or you can pay on the spot (although it is risky to go to a popular destination without a reservation). The *auberges* provide a bed and communal bathrooms and kitchens at very modest prices.

Chapter 4

Public Transportation

 Quels sont les horaires des trains? *(kel soh lay zo-rer day trih):* What are the train schedules?

France is very proud of its *SNCF,* the acronym for *Société Nationale des Chemins de Fer français.* This company manages fast and efficient trains to European destinations, and includes several high-speed *TGV* (*Train à Grande Vitesse*) lines and the *Eurotunnel* line linking France to England. Before taking any train, check timetables, prices, and tickets at a travel agency, a *syndicat d'initiative* (tourist office), or the Rail Europe website. Don't arrive late at the *gare* (train station) or you will surely miss your train. French trains are *vraiment ponctuels* (really on time). When you get to the station, look for an agent standing next to a big "i" (*informations*) sign. Agents usually speak English, as well as other languages. You can buy your tickets either at the *distributeurs automatiques* (ticket machines) in the station; they are computerized and very simple to use, or if you don't have cash or an appropriate *carte bancaire,* go to *le guichet* (ticket window). Make sure you are in the correct *queue* (line); there are different lines for local and long-distance travel. Buy your *billet* or *ticket* (ticket), and inspect it closely.

Find the correct *quai* (platform from which your train departs) on your ticket. Check the *panneau d'affichage* (announcement board) frequently in case there are schedule changes. Go to your *quai* well before the train is scheduled to leave. Look for a brightly colored, free-standing validation machine *pour composter votre billet* (to stamp [or punch] your ticket). This step is required before you get on the train.

Est-ce que c'est la queue pour les express?	Is this the line for express trains?
es keuh say la keuh poor lay zeks-pres	
Est-ce que c'est le quai numéro cinq?	Is this platform number five?
es keuh say leuh kay nU-may-ro sihk	
Est-ce que c'est la voie A ou B?	Is this track A or B?
es keuh say la vwa a oo bay	

 Un billet simple, s'il vous plaît! *(uh bee-yay sih-pl seel voo play)*: A one-way ticket, please!

If you're traveling one way, use this phrase when buying a ticket: *un billet simple, s'il vous plaît*. If you plan to come back to your starting point, ask for *un billet aller (et) retour*. French trains offer *première et deuxième classe* (first- and second-class) accommodations. Most trains offer *un wagon fumeur* (a smoking car) (but only in second class), dining cars (*wagons-restaurants*), as well as sleeping cars or sleepers (*wagons-lits*) on long-distance trips.

un billet aller (et) retour	a round-trip ticket
uh bee-yay a-lay (ay) reuh-toor	

un billet en première   a first-class ticket

uh bee-yay ah preuh-myer

un billet en deuxième   a second-class ticket

uh bee-yay ah deuh-zyem

un billet en non fumeur   a ticket in the non-smoking section

uh bee-yay ah noh fU-meuhr

 À quelle heure? *(a kel euhr):* At what time?/When?

French trains and public transportation in general run on very consistent and reliable schedules. It is important that you be *à l'heure* (on time) at the *gare* (train station) and that you give yourself enough time to read the huge display boards announcing *l'arrivée des trains* (train arrivals) and *le départ des trains* (train departures), as well as their *voies* (tracks) or *quais* (platforms). The tracks are often announced very close to arrival or departure times. If you are unsure about the arrival or departure time of a train, ask *À quelle heure arrive/part le train de/ pour Metz?* or *À quelle heure arrive/part le train de/ pour Nice?* (At what time does the train from/to Metz arrive/depart? or At what time does the train from/to Nice arrive/depart?)

À quelle heure arrive le train?   What time does the train arrive?

a kel euhr a-reev leuh trih

À quelle heure part le train?   What time does the train leave?

a kel euhr par leuh trih

 Où est ma place? *(oo ay ma plas):* Where is my seat?

A quintessential phrase for the tourist and traveler, the phrase *Où est... ?* (Where is . . . ?) can help you out of many situations. On the

25

train, looking for your reserved seat, show your ticket and ask: *Où est ma place?* (Where is my seat?) At the station, looking for the ticket booth, ask: *Où est le guichet des ventes?* (Where is the sales window?) Confused about the many tracks in a large train station like the *gare de l'Est*, ask: *Où est la voie pour le train de/pour Strasbourg?* (Where is the track for the train from/to Strasbourg?) Looking for the sleeping car, ask: *Où est le wagon-lit?* (Where is the sleeping car?) Looking for the conductor to check your ticket or to ask him a question, ask: *Où est le contrôleur?* (Where is the conductor?)

Où est le quai?	Where is the platform?
oo ay leuh kay	
Où est la voie pour le train de/ pour Strasbourg?	Where is the track for the train from/to Strasbourg?
oo ay la vwa poor leuh trih deuh/poor stras-boor	
Où est le wagon fumeur?	Where is the smoking car?
oo ay leuh va-goh fU-meuhr	
Où est le wagon-lit?	Where is the sleeping car?
oo ay leuh va-goh lee	
Où est le wagon-restaurant?	Where is the dining car?
oo ay leuh va-goh res-to-rah	
Où sont les horaires?	Where is the schedule?
oo soh lay zo-rer	
Où est le contrôleur/la contrôleuse?	Where is the conductor?
oo ay leuh koh-tro-leuhr/la koh-tro-leuhz	

Faut-il une réservation? *(fo teel Un ray-zer-va-syoh):* Do I need a reservation?

The *TGV* or *train à grande vitesse* (high-speed train) offers comfortable, rapid travel to many destinations. However, be sure to make *une réservation* (a reservation) as the TGV gets booked very rapidly. For travel on other long-distance trains, especially if you want a *couchette* (sleeping berth), also be sure to make a reservation.

Faut-il acheter/prendre le ticket   Do I have to buy the ticket ahead
   à l'avance?   of time?
fo-teel ash-tay/prah-dr leuh
   tee-kay a la-vahs

 Faut-il composter le ticket? *(fo-teel koh-pos-tay leuh tee-kay):* Do I have to validate the ticket?

Before boarding any train in France, look for *le composteur* (the automated validation box) which will punch or stamp *l'heure* (the time) and *la date* (the date) onto your ticket. If you don't see it, ask where it is: *Où est le composteur?* (Where is the validation machine?) Be sure to validate your ticket or you may be fined! Do not expect to see the conductor immediately upon boarding. Generally he will start his rounds either in the front or from the rear and work his way through the train after the train has started to move.

Où est le com posteur?   Where is the validation box?
oo ay leuh koh pos-teuhr

Est-ce qu'il y a un distributeur automatique de tickets?
(es keel ya uh dees-tree-bU-teuhr o-to-ma-teek deuh tee-kay): Is there a ticket machine?

The phrase *Il y a... ?* (Is there . . . ?) will come in handy when you are unsure of something. For example, if the ticket booth at the train or the subway station is closed, you might want to know if there is an automated ticket machine nearby. You'll use this phrase on the train, say, if you find a seat and want to be sure that it is not taken, or if you want to find out if there is a dining car.

Est-ce qu'il y a une place libre à côté de vous? es keel ya Un plas lee-br a ko-tay deuh voo	Is there an empty seat next to you?
Est-ce qu'il y a un wagon-restaurant dans ce train? es keel ya uh va-goh res-to-rah dah seuh trih	Is there a dining car on this train?

 Le vol est-il à l'heure? *(leuh vol ay-teel a leuhr):* Is the flight on time?

You are calling a French friend who is expecting you to confirm your flight arrival. Tell the person: *Mon vol est à l'heure* (moh vol ay ta leuhr). (My flight is on time.) You will probably get a surprised but relieved reaction such as: *Tant mieux!* (tah myeuh) (So much the better!/That's good!)

If, on the other hand, your flight has been delayed, say: *Le vol est remis* (leuh vol ay reuh-mee). If it has been canceled due to bad weather, say: *Mon vol est annulé à cause du mauvais temps* (moh vol ay ta-nU-lay a koz dU mo-vay tah). (My flight is canceled due to bad weather.)

If your flight has been overbooked, you will hear: *Le vol est sur-booké* (leuh vol ay sUr-boo-kay). If you agree to give up your seat for compensation, say: *Je veux bien céder ma place* (zheuh veuh byeh say-day ma plas).

Le vol arrive à quelle heure?
leuh vol a-reev a kel euhr
At what time does the flight arrive?

Le vol est annulé.
leuh vol ay ta-nU-lay
The flight is canceled.

Le vol est remis.
leuh vol ay reuh-mee
The flight is delayed.

Le vol est surbooké.
leuh vol ay sUr-boo-kay
The flight is overbooked.

 Il y a un vol direct pour Londres? *(eel ya uh vol dee-rekt poor loh-dr):* Is there a direct flight to London?

Use this question to find out if there is a direct flight to London. If you are told: *Le vol fait escale à Amsterdam*, then you will know that there is a layover in Amsterdam.

Le vol fait escale à Amsterdam.
leuh vol fay es-kal a am-ster-dam
The flight has a layover in Amsterdam.

Est-ce qu'il y a encore des places sur ce vol?
es keel ya ah-kor day plas sUr seuh vol
Are there any seats left on this flight?

Avez-vous une place en première?
a-vay voo Un plas ah preuh-myer
Do you have a seat in first class?

Est-ce que c'est l'autobus pour la gare? *(es keuh say lo-to-bUs poor la gar)*: Is this the bus for the train station?

All French cities have well-developed public transportation systems consisting of buses that run punctually and frequently from the city center to its suburbs. You can get a schedule of buses at a *syndicat d'initiative* (tourist office); it's usually also available online. Buses usually run from 6:30 A.M. to 8:30 P.M., and later in large cities. For example, Paris offers *le Noctambus* and *le Noctilien*, a nighttime bus service that links Paris to the suburbs.

If you need to go to the train station or to the airport with heavy bags, especially if you're on a budget, it may be easier to take a bus than a taxi (expensive) or the subway (many steep stairways). Before boarding the bus, be sure to ask *Est-ce que c'est l'autobus pour la gare/ pour l'aéroport?* (Is this the bus for the train station/the airport?)

Buses can also be a more relaxed and pleasurable way to enjoy the sights on your way downtown or to a museum. Again, make sure you are boarding the right bus by asking *Est-ce que c'est l'autobus pour le centre-ville?* (Is this the bus for downtown?) or *Est-ce que c'est le bus qui s'arrête au musée?* (Is this the bus that stops at the museum?)

Est-ce que c'est l'autobus pour la gare/l'aéroport?	Is this the bus for the train station/ the airport?
es keuh say lo-to-bUs poor la gar/ ay-ro-por	
Est-ce que c'est l'autobus pour le centre-ville?	Is this the bus for downtown?
es keuh say lo-to-bUs poor leuh sah-tr-veel	

Est-ce que c'est le bus qui s'arrête   Is this the bus that stops at
   au musée?   the museum?
es keuh say leuh bUs kee sa-ret
   o mU-zay

 Pouvez-vous me dire... ? *(poo-vay voo meuh deer):* Can you
tell me . . . ?

Should you be confused or uncertain, ask any bus driver for help. For
instance, if you are looking for the bus line to take you to the Arc de
Triomphe, place Charles de Gaulle, ask: *Pardon, Monsieur. Pouvez-vous
me dire où s'arrête le bus pour la place Charles de Gaulle?* (Excuse me,
sir. Can you tell me where the bus for the place Charles de Gaulle
stops?) If you are going to a less identifiable destination, ask the
driver: *Pouvez-vous me dire où je dois descendre pour... ?* (Can you tell
me where to get off for . . . ?)

Pouvez-vous me dire où s'arrête   Can you tell me where the bus for the
   le bus pour la place Charles   place Charles de Gaulle stops?
   de Gaulle?
poo-vay voo meuh deer oo sa-ret
   leuh bUs poor la plas sharl
   deuh gol
Pouvez-vous me dire où je dois   Can you tell me where to get off
   descendre pour... ?   for . . . ?
poo-vay voo meuh deer oo zheuh
   dwa day-sah-dreuh poor

C'est le bon arrêt. *(say leuh bo na-ray):* This is the right stop.

Every French bus stop has a sign that shows a five-digit code number, usually at the bottom. This code is useful in several ways: It lets you identify this stop as being the correct one for a bus line you may have been told to use. With the number in hand, you can phone the RATP to obtain the schedules of the buses that stop there.

While riding a bus, if you see that you are close to your destination, and you forgot to ring the bell, tell the driver: *C'est mon arrêt.* (This is my stop.) Or *C'est là que je descends.* (This is where I get off.)

C'est mon arrêt.	This is my stop.
say mo na-ray	
C'est là que je descends.	This is where I get off.
say la keuh zheuh day-sah	

 À quelle proximité d'une station de métro est l'hôtel? *(a kel prok-see-mee-tay dUn sta-syoh deuh may-tro ay lo-tel):* How close to a subway station is the hotel?

There are subway systems in six major French cities: Paris, Lille, Lyon, Marseille, Toulouse, and Rouen. They are generally open from 6:30 A.M. till 12:30 A.M. and trains run continuously as often as every two to three minutes during *les heures de pointe* (rush hours). In Paris, the subway system is a part of the *RATP* which includes subway trains, *RER* trains (linking Paris to its suburbs), and buses.

If you have a *métro* available, make sure to get information and maps ahead of time. Riding the *métro* will save you time and money. Before booking your hotel room, find out if the hotel is located near a subway station: *L'hôtel est-il près d'une station de métro?* or *À quelle proximité d'une station de métro est l'hôtel?*

L'hôtel est-il près d'une station de métro?	Is the hotel near a subway station?

lo-tel ay-teel pray dUn sta-syoh
    deuh may-tro

 Un billet, s'il vous plaît. *(uh bee-yay seel voo play):* One ticket, please.

Unlike bus tickets, which may be purchased on the bus, *métro* tickets must be purchased ahead of time at *les guichets* (ticket windows) or at *les distributeurs automatiques* (automated ticket machines) in the stations. Tickets are also available at *les kiosques* (newsstands) and in *les tabacs* (tobacco shops). It is more advantageous to buy *un carnet de tickets* (a book of tickets), usually ten at a time, rather than *un ticket/un aller simple* (a single ticket). Note that only *des cartes bancaires* (debit cards) and *des pièces* (coins) are accepted at the machines in some stations; it's always wise to carry change. Remember that the largest coins are two-euro coins.

In Paris, *métro* tickets are good for the subway system, as well as for the RER, and for bus and tramway rides within Paris (Zones 1 and 2 only); they include *les transferts* (transfers). You may transfer from the *métro* to the RER on a single ticket, but you must use a second ticket to transfer between the *métro*/RER and buses/tramways. The *métro* and the RER share a number of stations. Leaving an RER train, you'll need your ticket to exit the station. As a rule, always keep your *ticket composté* (validated ticket), in case an official asks to see it. Special tickets are required for buses and trains traveling to and from Paris regional airports.

Metro tickets (at the equivalent of $1.85 each) cost a little more individually than if purchased in a *carnet,* or book of ten. If you're going to be in Paris for a while, a *Carte Orange* (which is literally an orange card), an unlimited weekly pass on all buses and trains in Zones 1 and 2 (central Paris), is a less expensive alternative. You'll need a passport-size photograph when you buy your first *Carte Orange*.

C'est combien un carnet, s'il vous plaît? say koh-byeh uh kar-nay seel voo play	How much is a book of tickets, please?
Faites-moi une carte orange, s'il vous plaît. fet mwa Un kart o-rahzh seel voo play	Make me a weekly pass, please.

 Toujours en grève? *(too-zhoor ah grev):* Still on strike?

Remember that trade unions are very powerful in France and that transportation strikes are frequent and inevitable, especially during busy travel seasons. If you hear or read the question above, you will either have to show great patience or make alternative plans, as these strikes often last a long time. French *syndicats* (trade unions) are known for holding nationwide strikes that aim to protect transportation workers' benefits. Commuters are urged to postpone their trips, take the day off, or work from home. If you overhear *La route est bloquée par une manifestation* (la root ay blo-kay par Un ma-nee-fes-ta-syoh) (The road is blocked due to a protest), there is a good chance that there will also be drastically reduced train, bus, and subway service. Also be aware that during a transportation strike, top Parisian tourist attractions, including the Musée d'Orsay, the Louvre, and the palace of Versailles are often closed. So look in the newspaper, search online, or ask someone: *Le musée est fermé aujourd'hui?* (Is the museum closed today?)

Est-ce que la route est bloquée?   Is the road blocked?

es keuh la root ay blo-kay

Le musée est fermé aujourd'hui?   Is the museum closed today?

leuh mU-zay ay fer-may o-zhoor-dwee

 Quel est le tarif de location? *(kel ay leuh ta-reef deuh lo-ka-syoh):* What is the rental fee?

If you happen to be in Paris during a transportation strike, there may be only one subway train in ten running on most lines. This might be the right time to try out the capital's new *Velib* self-service bicycle rental. *Velib* stands for *vélo liberté* (bike freedom) and is a project of the city of Paris. Its slogan is *La ville est plus belle à vélo.* (The city is more beautiful from a bike.) So ask: *Quel est le tarif de location au service Velib?* (What is the rental charge at Velib?)

C'est le service Velib.   This is the Velib (citywide bike rental

say leuh ser-vees vay-leeb   service).

Quel est le tarif de location au   What is the rental charge at Velib?

service Velib?

kel ay leuh ta-reef deuh lo-ka-syoh

o ser-vees vay-leeb

 Taxi, s'il vous plaît! *(tak-see seel voo play):* Taxi, please!

Although you will probably try to avoid taking taxis during rush hour in Paris, you may still have to rely on them to get back to your hotel on a late evening out, especially since the *métro* closes at 1 A.M. The best way to get a cab is to ask the *concierge* of a hotel or restaurant to call one for you. Use the phrase *Taxi, s'il vous plaît* while offering a *pourboire* (tip) to the *concierge* or restaurant host. In spite of the horror stories you may have been told about Parisian cab drivers, you should know that Parisian taxi rates are the lowest in France and among the three lowest in the European community. The *Préfecture de Police de Paris* sets rigorous standards for *les chauffeurs de taxi* (taxi drivers). If you need to take a taxi from the airport, make sure to go outside and *faire la queue* (wait in line) near the spaces reserved for taxis outside the arrival terminals. Expect a surcharge for luggage.

Quelle est la surcharge pour les bagages?	What is the surcharge for luggage?

kel ay la sUr-sharzh poor lay ba-gazh

Chapter 5

Driving

 Pourrais-je avoir un autre modèle? *(poo-rezh a-vwar euh no-tr mo-del)*: Can I get another model?

Driving through small French towns and villages will give you a totally different perspective on the French and France. For that, you'll have to rent a car. Although you will most likely arrange your rental from home, upon picking up your car, you may need to ask the attendant if you can get an upgrade, perhaps *un autre modèle* (a different model), or *une voiture plus grande* (a bigger car). Remember that French roads tend to be narrower than in North America, and that in small towns or in the oldest quarters of bigger towns and cities, streets will be very narrow.

Pourrais-je avoir une voiture plus grande?	Can I get a bigger car?
poo-rezh a-vwar Un vwa-tUr plU grahd	
Pourrais-je avoir un autre modèle?	Can I get another model?
poo-rezh a-vwar euh no-tr mo-del	

Est-ce que cette voiture consomme du diesel? *(es keuh set vwa-tUr koh-som dU dee-zel):* Does that car use diesel?

Most French cars are small by American standards (although minivans are available), and they are mostly very economical. If you rent a car that runs on diesel, you will save a good deal on fuel, because the mileage is quite high. When you refuel, you will notice that gas is sold by the liter (at approximately four liters to the gallon); so do not misinterpret the posted price of French gasoline which will look low to you. If it is 2 euros per liter, that would be about 8 euros per gallon.

Quelle sorte d'essence est-ce que je dois acheter?	What kind of gas do I have to buy?
kel sort de-sahs es keuh zheuh dwa ash-tay	
Est-ce que je dois faire le plein avant de rendre la voiture?	Do I fill it up before returning the car?
es keuh zheuh dwa fer leuh plih a-vah deuh rah-dr la vwa-tUr	

 C'est à combien de kilomètres d'ici, la prochaine ville? *(say ta koh-byeh deuh kee-lo-metr dee-see la pro-shen veel):* How many kilometers from here is the next town?

Once you are on the road, you will be driving through the French countryside, and the experience will be very much like driving in the U.S., except for the posted speeds. France is on the metric system, therefore all speed limits are posted in *kilomètres/heure* (kilometers per hour [km/h]). One kilometer is 0.6 of a mile; therefore, 100 kilometers per hour equals approximately 60 miles per hour. You will need to watch not only the posted speed limits but also your car's odometer.

Many *autoroutes* (highways) allow speeds of 130 km/h. When driving through villages, you will slow down to 50 km/h.

Quelle est la limite de vitesse?   What is the speed limit?

kel ay la lee-meet deuh vee-tes

 Quelle rue est-ce? *(kel rU es):* Which street is it?

In cities or towns, the three-letter word *rue* (rU) (street) could become your biggest headache. Make sure to have a good road map as well as a city map with you, and study them carefully. French streets may change names every block, and the signs that tell what street you're on are usually not on posts (where we might look for them), but on buildings or even on corner houses! In addition, streets are often named after famous people or events. So be ready to make frequent use of the word *rue* as you ask: *La rue Jean-Jaurès, quelle rue est-ce?* (la rU zhah zho-res, kel rU es) (Jean-Jaurès Street, which street is it?)

Les avenues, which usually converge toward the center of town, and *les boulevards*, which tend to circle towns and cities, are a little easier to locate because they are major roadways.

Also, you will find *ronds-points* (traffic circles) everywhere in France; it has been estimated that there are approximately 20,000 of them in the country. The most famous *rond-point* is most likely the *rond-point des Champs-Élysées* in Paris. The purpose of these circles is to force every car approaching an intersection to slow down, so there is no question as to which has priority. The *ronds-points* are often covered with beautiful flower beds or other artistic ornaments, making them small works of art. Another useful term is *pont* (bridge); there are so many of them because many French towns were originally built along a river. French bridges such as *le pont d'Avignon* or *le Pont-Neuf* have been made famous in songs and poems. Finally, if you are driving through small villages, watch out for *sentiers* (footpaths) or *allées* (alleys), especially if you are driving a larger car; only the natives know how to drive on these narrow passageways.

 Est-ce qu'il y a un parking? *(es keel ya uh par-keeng)*: Is there a parking garage?

When driving a car in a big city, you should definitely find out if there is adequate parking at the site or store you are planning to visit. It will be a relief to you if the *grand magasin* (department store) has underground parking (even if parking is subject to a fee).

Le grand magasin a un parking souterrain.	The department store has underground parking.
leuh grah ma-ga-zih a uh par-keeng soo-tay-rih	
Le parking, est-il payant?	Is there a fee for parking?
leuh par-keeng ay teel pay-yah	

 Est-ce que c'est une route à péage? *(es keuh say tUn root a pay-yazh)*: Is it a toll road?

Superhighways, known as *autoroutes*, are normally toll roads. Secondary national highways are indicated on maps by an N or RN for *Route Nationale*. Often the most scenic, the *Routes Départementales* (maintained by local governments) are indicated by the letter D. Highways in France tend to be jammed in late July and August, the most popular months for the French to vacation. Plan accordingly!

Je suis perdu(e). *(zheuh swee per-dU):* I am lost.

Je suis perdu(e) is a phrase you will almost surely use if you decide to rent a car and drive it through France's beautiful countryside. *Attention!* (Careful!) Roads are narrow, most often two-lane, and *les panneaux* (road signs) only show the direction from one town to another, unlike the United States where signs generally also indicate the direction you're traveling. Therefore, in order to drive in France, it is practically imperative that you know the names of all the towns between your point of departure and your destination. *Attention!* (Careful!) If you decide to stop at one of the numerous cafés along the way to ask directions, be ready to spend a long time waiting for the customers to argue among themselves as to *la meilleure route à prendre* (the best road to take) or about *Quelle est la direction à prendre?* (What direction should we take?)

Quelle est la meilleure route à prendre?	What is the best road to take?
kel ay la may-euhr root a prah-dr	
Quelle est la direction à prendre?	Which direction should we take?
kel ay la dee-rek-syoh a prah-dr	

 Vos papiers, s'il vous plaît. *(vo pa-pyay seel voo play):* Your papers, please.

If another motorist flashes his/her lights on a country road, this may mean: *Attention au gendarme!* (Watch out for a patrolman!) Even though it is illegal to flash these warnings, the French do it anyway. In the event that you are stopped by *a gendarme*, be sure to carry your *passeport* (passport), *permis de conduire* (driver's license), *papiers de l'assurance* (insurance documents), and *enregistrement* (car registra-

41

tion) at all times. Your driver's license from home will be sufficient, though some tourists carry a one-year international driver's license (available at your automobile association).

Following a government initiative, there have recently been more and more *contrôles sur la route* (road checks) with *tests de sobriété sur place* (sobriety spot checks). This is quite common, especially in rural areas. If you are stopped, always be polite, and address the policeman as *monsieur l'agent* (meuh-syeuh la-zhah) or *monsieur le gendarme* (meuh-syeuh leuh zhah-darm) and present your *papiers* (papers).

Votre permis de conduire, s'il vous plaît.	Your driver's license, please.
vot per-mee deuh koh-dweer seel voo play	
Attention à l'agent de police!	Watch out for the policeman!
a-tah-syoh a la-zahn deuh po-lees	
Attention au contrôle!	Watch out for a road check!
a-tah-syoh o koh-trol	
Attention aux tests de sobriété sur place!	Watch out for sobriety tests on the spot!
a-tah-syoh o test deuh so-bree-yay-tay sUr plas	

 Vous avez une amende. *(voo za-vay Un a-mahd):* You have a fine.

Sooner or later, this unwelcome phrase is sure to be heard by traffic offenders in France. Radar traps are frequent, and speed limits rigorously enforced. If you break the law you can expect to be fined if the *gendarmes* stop you. *Les amendes*, also called *contraventions* (traffic tickets), can vary from approximately 30 to over 3,000 euros for serious *excès de vitesse* (speeding), or even more for *conduite en état d'ivresse* (drunk driving). Nonresidents must pay fines *en espèces* (in cash) on the spot.

Vous avez une amende pour excès de vitesse.	You have a fine for speeding.
voo za-vay Un a-mahd poor ek-say deuh vee-tes	
Vous avez une contravention pour conduite en état d'ivresse.	You have a fine for drunk driving.
voo za-vay Un koh-tra-vah-syoh poor koh-dweet ah nay-ta dee-vres	

 Vous connaissez le code de la route? *(voo ko-nes-say leuh kod deuh la root):* Do you know the rules of the road?

A law that is more and more strictly enforced in France prohibits talking on a *portable* (cell phone) while driving. Article R412-6-1 of the *code de la route* (rules of the road) stipulates that it is forbidden to use a handheld phone while driving. To disregard this law is punishable with a fine of 150 euros (22 euros if paid within three days) and two points on your *permis de conduire* (driver's license). *Un kit mains-libres* (a hands-free headset) is tolerated as long as the driver uses good judgment.

Another law that is worth being aware of is *la priorité à droite* (yield to the right). This law gives the right of way to motorists turning onto your road in the direction you are traveling, from the right.

In an effort to alleviate traffic, many French cities now encourage the use of bicycles by natives as well as tourists. Paris promotes its *Velib* program (bike rental stations throughout the city). If you decide to rent a bicycle, be aware that *le code de la route* also applies to bicyclists as do fines for running a red light or any other infraction. An article published in *Le Monde* in April 2007 says: "À Paris, ils [les cyclistes] ne bénéficient officiellement d'aucun traitement de faveur." (In Paris, they [cyclists] do not enjoy any favorable treatment.) The city of Strasbourg, in a progressive move, installed *des contresens cyclables* (bike lanes) in its historic center. Cycling associations are currently lobbying to obtain modified laws for cyclists; meanwhile, however, *respectez le code de la route* (follow the same rules you would follow as a motorist) when you ride a bike in the city.

Il faut respecter la priorité à droite. You must yield to the right.
eel fo res-pek-tay la pree-o-ree-tay

a drwat

 Je cherche une station service. *(zheuh shersh Un sta-syoh ser-vees):* I am looking for a gas station.

Look for new types of fuel next time you're driving in France and pull up to a *pompe à essence* (gas pump). Stations are increasingly selling *l'essence5*, a fuel composed of 95 percent unleaded gas and 5 percent ethanol. The advantage of this fuel is that it does not require any modifications to the car. Another fuel which has appeared on the market is called *l'E85*; it is produced with renewable resources and emits four times less carbon monoxide than traditional gasoline. While most gas stations are now self-serve, you may still need to use the following expression if you give your credit card to the attendant. Say: *Je veux faire le plein.* (zheuh veuh fer leuh plih) (I want to fill it up.)

If you happen to get in trouble on an *autoroute* (highway), try to stop at the first gas station you see and ask the attendant to check your oil: *Vérifiez l'huile, s'il vous plaît!* (Check the oil, please!) or *Changez le pneu arrière/avant* (Change the rear/front tire). If you need a road map, you'll find *cartes routières* in supermarkets, bookstores, and at gas stations and highway rest stops.

La pompe à essence ne fonctionne pas. la pohp a es-sahs neuh fohk-syon pa	The gas pump does not work.
Je veux faire le plein. zheuh veuh fer leuh plih	I want to fill it up.
Vérifiez l'huile, s'il vous plaît! vay-ree-fyay lweel seel voo play	Check the oil, please!
Changez le pneu arrière/avant, s'il vous plaît! shah-zhay leuh pneuh a-ryer/a-vah seel voo play	Change the rear/front tire, please!
Une carte routière, s'il vous plaît! Un kart root-yer seel voo play	A road map, please!

Chapter 6

Shopping

 **Quel grand magasin me conseilleriez-vous?** *(kel grah ma-ga-zih meuh koh-say-yeuh-ryay voo):* What department store would you recommend?

To tourists' delight, French cities are amazingly appealing to all kinds of shoppers. Do you want *des objets de luxe* (luxury items)? Head for the *place Vendôme* and the *avenue Montaigne*. Shopping for clothes and personal items? In that case, head for the *grands magasins* (this phrase translates literally as "big stores"), like the famous *Galeries Lafayette* and *Le Printemps*. Regardless of where you are staying, you will want to *faire du shopping* (do some shopping); so ask anyone at your hotel to direct you to a *grand magasin* or to neighborhoods where boutiques and outdoor stands abound.

Or perhaps all you want to do today is walk through the streets of Paris and look at the beautiful display windows. In that case, you will be indulging in *le lèche-vitrine* (window-shopping)! The literal meaning of *lèche-vitrine* is "window-licking," probably because of the delicious appeal of the displays.

Dans quel quartier est-ce qu'il y a des boutiques de haute couture?

dah kel kar-tyay es keel ya day boo-teek deuh ot koo-tUr

In what neighborhood are there designer boutiques?

Dans quels quartiers est-ce qu'on trouve des antiquaires?

dah kel kar-tyay es koh troov day zah-tee-ker

In what neighborhoods do you find antiques shops?

 Où est le rayon de vêtements pour dames? *(oo ay leuh ray-oh deuh vet-mah poor dam):* Where is the women's department?

Looking for the women's department, ask: *Où est le rayon de vêtements pour dames?* If it happens to be a few floors up, ask for the escalator or the elevator by saying *Où est l'escalier roulant?* or *Où est l'ascenseur?* Found something you liked and ready to try it on? Ask: *Où est le salon d'essayage?* Completed your purchases and looking for the checkout register, ask: *Où est la caisse, s'il vous plaît?*

Où est le rayon de vêtements pour hommes?

oo ay leuh ray-oh deuh vet-mah poor om

Where is the men's department?

Où est le rayon sport?

oo ay leuh ray-oh spor

Where is the sportswear department?

Où est le rayon des chaussures?

oo ay leuh ray-oh day sho-sUr

Where is the shoe department?

Où est l'ascenseur?

oo ay la-sah-seuhr

Where is the elevator?

Où est le salon d'essayage?   Where is the fitting room?

oo ay leuh sa-loh des-say-azh

Où est la caisse?   Where is the checkout register?

oo ay la kes

 Où est le service détaxe? *(oo ay leuh ser-vees day-tax):* Where is the duty-free department?

When shopping for expensive items in a department store, be sure to stop at the duty-free desk. The French pay high sales taxes on many purchases. Tourists must fulfill certain requirements, including getting purchase verification from the store. They then deposit the paperwork at the airport when they leave the country and will eventually be reimbursed the amount of tax paid. This procedure can save you a good deal of money on expensive purchases. Smaller stores will also honor your request for *détaxe* as long as you satisfy the minimum purchase price.

Pouvez-vous me donner les   Can you give me the duty-free
   documents de détaxe?   documentation?

poo-vay voo meuh do-nay lay
   do-ku-mah deuh day-tax

 Avez-vous... ? *(a-vay voo):* Do you have . . . ?

This is the quintessential phrase for shopping: it can be used to ask for a size, a color, a brand, or a model. When shopping for clothes, ask: *Avez-vous une taille 38*? (Do you have a size 38?) For shoes, ask: *Avez-vous ces chaussures en noir*? (Do you have these shoes in black?) At a café, you might ask: *Avez-vous du thé à la menthe*? (Do you have mint tea?)

When you go to bakery, don't be afraid to ask: *Qu'avez-vous de spécial aujourd'hui?* (What is special today?) Oftentimes, small businesses such as bakeries take great pride in offering seasonal specialties: rhubarb tarts, for example, when rhubarb is in season, as well as weekly or daily specials.

Qu'avez-vous dans cette taille?   What do you have in this size?
ka-vay voo dah set tay
L'avez-vous en noir?   Do you have it in black?
la-vay voo ah nwar
Qu'avez-vous de spécial?   What specials do you have?
ka-vay voo deuh spay-syal

 Je voudrais... *(zheuh voo-dray):* I would like . . .

Always remember that the French are *à cheval sur les manières*, which means that they have an obsession about respecting good manners; in other words, they expect everyone to be courteous. Since French and Americans often have different concepts of courtesy, each may find the other rude at times. When an American walks into a shop and simply starts looking around without first saying *Bonjour, Madame* or *Bonjour, Monsieur*, the French find that quite rude. Therefore it is important to use polite phrases with everyone and treat employees, shopkeepers, and waiters, not as friends, but as professionals.

Do you want coffee and croissants for breakfast before setting out for your day of shopping? Say: *Bonjour, Monsieur. Je voudrais un café crème avec des croissants, s'il vous plaît* instead of an imperative and authoritarian sounding *Je veux...* (I want . . .). *Je voudrais*, the "would like" phrase, echoes a polite *Qu'est-ce que je peux vous servir?* (kes keuh zheuh peuh voo ser-veer) (What may I serve you?)

Looking for that special Dior lipstick, ask: *Je voudrais un rouge à lèvres Dior.* If you would like to have it gift-wrapped, here is the phrase to use: *Je voudrais un paquet-cadeau, s'il vous plaît.* Or if you want to sound even more French, tell the salesperson that it is *pour offrir* (this means you're offering it to someone as a gift).

Je voudrais un rouge à lèvres Dior. I would like a Dior lipstick.
zheuh voo-dray uh roozh a levr
   dee-yor

Je voudrais un café crème. I would like a coffee with cream.
zheuh voo-dray uh ka-fay krem

Je voudrais un paquet-cadeau. I would like to have it gift-wrapped.
zheuh voo-dray uh pa-kay ka-do

C'est pour offrir. It is a gift.
say poor o-freer

 J'aimerais… *(zhem-ray)*   *I would like . . .*

J'aimerais is a synonym for *Je voudrais* that is less emphatic. You are simply stating your preference without insisting. You may use it, for example, to ask for a table by the window or to suggest the Galeries Lafayette instead of a different store.

If you want a large grocery store, ask where you can find a *Francprix* or *Monoprix*, two chains of *supermarchés* (supermarkets). Expect these stores to be somewhat impersonal compared to family-owned shops. Also, in the large stores, expect to bag your own groceries. On the other hand, when you're shopping for fresh produce at one of the many outdoor stands or small grocery stores, be aware that you will anger the salesperson or the owner if you touch the produce with your own hands. You will probably be reprimanded with a stern *Ne touchez pas, Monsieur/Madame!* (neuh too-shay pa meuh-syeuh/ma-dam) (Don't touch, Sir/Madam!) To avoid such confrontations, always tell the clerk what you want; for example, say: *J'aimerais un melon un peu mûr* (I would like a medium-ripe melon) or *un melon très mûr* (a very ripe melon). You can also tell the salesperson when you plan to eat the produce and he/she will carefully choose the right degree of ripeness for you. Note that some small stores now provide plastic bags—along with disposable gloves—which you must don before choosing your produce.

J'aimerais une table à côté de la fenêtre.	I would like a table next to the window.
zhem-ray Un ta-bl a ko-tay deuh la feuh-ne-tr	
J'aimerais aller aux Galeries Lafayette.	I would like to go to the Galeries Lafayette.
zhem-ray a-lay o gal-ree la-fa-yet	
J'aimerais un melon très mûr.	I would like a very ripe melon.
zhem-ray uh meuh-loh tray mUr	
J'aimerais un melon pour ce soir.	I would like a melon for tonight.
zhem-ray uh meuh-loh poor seuh swar	

 Je cherche des chaussures. *(zheuh shersh day sho-sUr):* I am looking for shoes.

French shoes may seem outrageously expensive, but they will undoubtedly be noticed back in the United States for their unique-ness and their *cachet*. However, it is not impossible to find *des chaussures bon marché* (inexpensive shoes) in areas frequented by students and young people, for example, on and around the *boulevard St-Michel* in the Latin Quarter. Depending on the time of year and your shoe size, you may or may not be able to find those unique and stunning shoes you imagine showing off back home. What you can count on, however, is that skilled salespeople are adept at sizing you up and will no doubt find you the right size if it is available. So, after the customary *Excusez-moi*, do not hesitate to ask for help, and use the phrase *Je cherche*.

Je cherche des chaussures bon marché.	I am looking for reasonably priced shoes.
zheuh shersh day sho-sUr boh mar-shay	
Je cherche des chaussures haut de gamme.	I am looking for high-quality shoes.
zheuh shersh day sho-sUr o deuh gam	
Je cherche cette chaussure dans ma pointure.	I am looking for this shoe in my size.
zheuh shersh set sho-sUr dah ma pwih-tUr	
Je cherche une paire de bottes noires.	I am looking for a pair of black boots.
zheuh shersh Un per deuh bot nwar	

 Il me faut... *(eel meuh fo):* I need . . .

Forgot something on your shopping spree? Perhaps a bottle of perfume? Quickly add: *Il me faut* or *Il me faudrait aussi un flacon de parfum*. The phrase *Il me faut* will convey that you have an absolute necessity for the item you're asking for: you must have it. If you would rather not sound so desperate, use the phrase *Il me faudrait* instead of *Il me faut*. The conditional mood of the verb *falloir* (*il me faudrait*) helps temper the urgency of the request. If, on the contrary, you want to stress the urgency of your need, say: *Il me faut absolument…*

Il me faudrait encore une chose.   I could use one more thing.
eel meuh fo-dray ah-kor Un shoz
Il me faut absolument...   I absolutely must have . . .
eel meuh fo ab-so-lU-mah

 Ça fait combien? *(sa fay koh-byeh):* How much is it?

Another quintessential phrase for shopping is *Ça fait combien?* This phrase has many synonyms such as *Combien ça fait?*, *C'est combien?*, and *Combien ça coûte?* (How much is it?) Use any one of them whenever a price is not posted or you are not sure what the price is. Learn to recognize the sign for the euro which will appear on *l'étiquette* (the price tag) of your merchandise; a price of 20 euros will appear as follows: 20€.

Combien est-ce que ça fait?   How much is it?/What's the total bill?
koh-byeh es keuh sa fay
C'est combien?   How much is it?
say koh-byeh
Combien est-ce que ça coûte?   How much does it cost?
koh-byeh es keuh sa koot

C'est très cher. *(say tray sher)*: It is very expensive.

The French love their *marchés* (outdoor markets, such as flower and produce markets), *bouquinistes* (used-book stalls), *marchés aux puces* (flea markets), and *brocantes* (yard sales). The latter can be home yard sales, also called *vide-greniers* (emptying the attic). Block-wide yard sales called *les brocantes de quartier* are often held as well. At all those places, it is expected that you will *marchander* (bargain) with the merchant or the seller. It is fun and it is part of the experience. Even *les antiquaires* (antiques dealers) are usually open to bargaining. So if you do not like the price, simply say *C'est très cher* (It's very expensive), *C'est trop cher* (It's too expensive), or even *C'est pas donné. Faites-moi un prix, s'il vous plaît.* (That's not cheap. Please give me a better price.)

C'est trop cher.	It is too expensive.
say tro sher	
C'est pas donné.	That's not cheap.
say pa don-nay	
Faites-moi un prix.	Give me a better price.
fet mwa uh pree	

 C'est une aubaine. *(say tUn o-ben)*: This is (You're getting) a great deal.

If, while you're bargaining at a *marché aux puces* (flea market) or a *brocanterie* (yard sale), the seller tells you *C'est une aubaine* or *C'est une bonne affaire*, he/she is trying to persuade you that you are getting a good deal. Should the seller be happy with your offer, he/she might say: *C'est parfait* (That's perfect) or *Bon, ça va* (That's fine) or *Marché conclu* (Done deal).

C'est une bonne affaire.	It's a good deal.
say tUn bon a-fer	
C'est parfait.	That's perfect.
say par-fay	
Bon, ça va.	That's fine.
boh sa va	
Marché conclu.	Done deal.
mar-shay koh-klU	

 Je peux l'essayer? *(zheuh peuh les-say-yay)*: May I try it on?

Have you found the dress or shirt you've been dreaming of and want to try it on? Ask the salesperson: *Je peux l'essayer?* (May I try it on?) Don't be intimidated when you decide to look at or try on clothes in Parisian boutiques. Understand that salespeople, in small clothing stores especially, are often very attentive and may even seem a little high pressure. Don't be surprised if they give you "the look" after you've tried something on and not purchased it. However, try to avoid going into a boutique just to browse; this may not be appreciated. Store personnel expect serious clients.

Love your choice? Say: *Je le/la prends.* (I am taking it.) Then ask if you can pay with a check or a credit card: *Je peux payer avec un chèque ou une carte de crédit?* If you decide a few days later that your purchase was not a good choice, you can return or exchange it; to return it and get your money back, use the phrase: *Est-ce que je peux me faire rembourser?*

Je peux payer avec un chèque ou une carte de crédit?	May I pay with a check or a credit card?
zheuh peuh pay-yay a-vek uh shek oo Un kart deuh kray-dee	
Je peux me faire rembourser?	Can I get my money back?
zheuh peuh meuh fer rah-boor-say	
Je le/la prends.	I'll take it.
zheuh leuh/la prah	

 Ça me plaît. *(sa meuh play)*: I like it.

Use *ça me plaît* whenever you like something—anything at all: *Une soirée au théâtre? Ah oui, ça me plaît! Quelle bonne idée!* (An evening at the theater? I like it! What a good idea!)

Save *Je l'aime* for a person (I like/I love him/her). *Je l'aime* is rarely used for things unless it is modified by an adverb, as in: *Je l'aime beaucoup* or *Je l'aime bien.* On the other hand, *Il/Elle me plaît* can be used for things or for people. Just be aware that saying *Il me plaît* about a man or *Elle me plaît* about a woman implies one is attracted romantically to him/her. Finally, if you see something you absolutely love, say *Je l'adore.* If you do not like it at all, say *Ça ne me plaît pas du tout.*

Ça me plaît beaucoup.	I like it a lot.
sa meuh play bo-koo	
Je l'aime beaucoup.	I like it a lot.
zheuh lem bo-koo	
Je l'adore.	I love it.
zheuh la-dor	

Il/Elle me plaît.	I like it. *or* I'm attracted to him/to her.
eel/el meuh play	
Ça ne me plaît pas du tout.	I don't like it at all.
sa neuh meuh play pa dU too	

 Ça me va? *(sa meuh va)*: Does it fit me?/Does it suit me?

You can use *Ça me va?* when seeking someone's opinion or advice while you're trying on clothes. You can also use it (but not as a question) to acknowledge that something does fit you and you are ready to buy it by saying: *Ça me va; je le/la prends.* If it doesn't fit, say: *Ça ne me va pas.*

You can also add adverbs to this phrase, as in: *Ça me va bien/très bien.* (It fits me well/very well.)

Ça me va bien/très bien.	It fits/suits me well/very well.
sa meuh va byeh/tray byeh	
Je le/la prends.	I am taking it.
zheuh leuh/la prah	
Ça ne me va pas.	It does not fit/suit me.
sa neuh meuh va pa	

 Est-ce que c'est en solde? *(es keuh say tah sold)*:
Is it on sale?

Les soldes (sales) are a huge commercial event mandated by the French government. They take place twice a year, in January and June, when the government allows stores to sell out their seasonal stock at much-discounted prices. *Les soldes* are so popular and stir up so much anticipation that some stores stage special midnight openings (much like Black Friday, the day after Thanksgiving in the United States). Stores are only allowed to mark down *les prix* (prices) for new items that were marked at the original price for at least a month before the sale starts. So be careful and examine *les étiquettes* (tags). When in doubt, always ask *Est-ce que cet article est soldé?* (Is this item on sale?), or *Est-ce que le prix sur l'étiquette est le prix soldé?* (Is the price on the tag the sale price?)

Est-ce que cet article est soldé?	Is this item on sale?
es keuh set ar-tee-kl ay sol-day	
Où est l'étiquette?	Where is the tag?
oo ay lay-tee-ket	
Est-ce que c'est le prix soldé?	Is this the sale price?
es keuh say leuh pree sol-day	
Est-ce que le prix sur l'étiquette est le prix soldé?	Is the price on the tag the sale price?
es keuh leuh pree sUr lay-tee-ket ay leuh pree sol-day	

 C'est à la mode. *(say ta la mod)*: This is in style.

It is very important for a French person to be true to him- or herself and at the same time *à la mode* (in style). This is where ingenuity plays a big role. The way you dress must meet the double standard of expressing your *soi* (individuality) and fitting into *la dernière mode* (the latest fashion). French women are known experts at finding the correct belt, the unique piece of jewelry, or the right scarf to create a certain "look" (*avoir le look*). The fact that there are several words for "scarf" (*le fichu*: small neckerchief; *l'écharpe*: shawl; *le foulard*: silk scarf) indicates the important role it plays. Well conceived and carefully selected accessories give a special updated *cachet* to an otherwise classic outfit.

Often, in fashion, certain styles such as *la longueur de la robe* (dress length) are brought back into style: *un style est remis au goût du jour.* If you come across: "*La Redoute multiplie les mini-collections pour être dans le vent,*" interpret this ad copy as: "*Redoute* (the online department store) expands its mini-collections to stay up-to-date."

C'est à la dernière mode.	It is in style (with emphasis on the
say ta la der-nyer mod	latest style).
remis au goût du jour	back in style
reuh-mee o goo dU zhoor	
être dans le vent	to be up-to-date/to be "in"
etr dah leuh vah	
avoir le look	to have the (right) look
a-vwar leuh "look"	

 C'est démodé. *(say day-mo-day):* It's out of fashion.

With modern awareness that luxury items such as fur coats and accessories often reflect cruel treatment of animals, *les manteaux de fourrure naturelle sont démodés* (natural fur coats are out of fashion). If you overhear *Les pelisses en vison, ça ne se voit presque plus* (lay peuh-lees ah vee-soh sa neuh seuh vwa pres-keuh plU), this means: Mink stoles are hardly around anymore. If you hear *Les pantalons à pattes d'éléphant, ça ne se fait plus* (lay pah-ta-loh a pat day-lay-fah sa neuh seuh fay plU), you heard: Bell-bottom pants just aren't done anymore. If you really want to be sarcastic about how dated something is, say: *Ça date de la préhistoire.* (That goes back to prehistoric times.)

C'est vieux jeu.   It's old-fashioned.

say vyeuh zheuh

Ça ne se voit plus.   It's not around anymore.

sa neuh seuh vwa plU

Ça ne se fait plus.   It's not done anymore.

sa neuh seuh fay plU

Ça date de la préhistoire.   That goes back to prehistoric times.

sa dat deuh la pray-ees-twar

 Ça, c'est du dernier cri. *(sa say dU der-nyay kree)*:
That's/This is the latest style.

Style and fashion extend beyond clothes into areas such as la *technologie médiatique* (media technology). How important is it for a French adolescent to carry *un portable du dernier cri* (latest model cell phone)? You can venture to say that it is just as vital as in the United States for him/her to be *dans le coup* (to be "in") or *branché(e)* (plugged in/connected). Note the double technology-oriented meaning of the phrase *être branché(e)* which can literally mean being connected via informational devices, but also has the figurative meaning of being "in the loop," keeping up with the latest technological progress.

Interpret the sentence *Tu as un ordinateur avec la capacité du dernier cri; tu es vraiment dans le coup,* as follows: You have a computer with the most updated capacity; you really are in on things.

Tu as un ordinateur avec la capacité du dernier cri; tu es vraiment dans le coup.
tU a euh nor-dee-na-teuhr a-vek la ka-pa-see-tay dU der-nyay kree tU ay vray-mah dah leuh coo

You have a computer with the most updated capacity; you really are in on things.

 Ça ne marche pas. *(sa neuh marsh pa):* It doesn't work.

This all-purpose phrase will prove useful on many occasions. It has nothing to do with "marching" or "walking," but rather means that something does not work. *Mon portable ne marche pas* (moh por-ta-bl neuh marsh pa) means that your cell phone is not working. If that is the case, you will want to exchange it immediately, saying: *Je voudrais l'échanger.* (I would like to exchange it.) Did you buy a pretty new phone in France and find out later it won't be compatible with our phone systems in the United States? That's too bad! *Il n'est pas compatible.* (It is not compatible.) You are using a computer at a *cybercafé*, but for some reason are unable to get onto the Web; tell the person in charge: *Quelque chose ne va pas.* (Something is not right.)

Quelque chose ne va pas.
kel-keuh shoz neuh va pa

Something is not right.

Il n'est pas compatible.
eel nay pa koh-pa-tee-bl

It is not compatible.

Je voudrais l'échanger.
zheuh voo-dray lay-shah-zhay

I would like to exchange it.

Voilà le reçu. *(vwa-la leuh reuh-sU):* Here's/There's the receipt.

In case you have to return an appliance or anything else you purchased, remember to bring your *reçu* (receipt) to the store. Also hand over all documentation that came with the item to be returned: *Voilà/ Voici les papiers!* (Here are the papers!)

Voilà les papiers.   Here/There are the papers.

vwa-la lay pa-pyay

Je voudrais échanger cet article défectueux. *(zheuh voo-dray ay-shah-zhay set ar-tee-kl day-fek-tU-euh):* I would like to exchange this defective item.

If you are dissatisfied with a purchase, there are several scenarios that may ensue. You may just want to return the item and get your money back. In that case, say: *Je voudrais qu'on me rembourse.* (I would like to be reimbursed.) You may prefer to hold on to your item if it can be repaired; in that case, say: *Je voudrais qu'on me répare cela.* (I would like to have this repaired.) Or you may prefer to exchange the item; in that case, say: *Je voudrais échanger cet article défectueux.* (I would like to exchange this defective item.) If you do not get satisfaction when returning a defective product, ask to speak to *le gérant* (the manager).

Je voudrais qu'on me répare cela.   I would like to have this repaired.

zheuh voo-dray koh meuh ray-par
   seuh-la

Je voudrais qu'on me rembourse. I would like to be reimbursed.

zheuh voo-dray koh meuh rah-boors

Puis-je parler à quelqu'un d'autre? May I talk to someone else?

pweesh par-lay a kel-kuh dotr

Puis-je parler avec le gérant? May I speak with the manager?

pweesh par-lay a-vek leuh zhay-rah

Chapter 7

Grooming

 Pouvez-vous m'indiquer le rayon des articles de toilette?
(poo-vay voo mih-dee-kay leuh ray-yoh day zar-tee-kl deuh twa-let):
Can you direct me to the toiletries department?

You may shop for toiletries in a French pharmacy, drugstore, or department store. In large stores, ask for *les articles de toilette.* You will find many different brands of *les déodorants* (deodorants), *les parfums* (perfumes), *l'eau de Cologne* (colognes), *les shampooing* (shampoos), *les crèmes à raser* (shaving creams), *le maquillage* (makeup), and other personal items. Remember that electrical appliances such as hair dryers require 220 to 240 volts in France (110 to 120 volts in the United States). Do not try to use the hair dryer you brought from home without an appropriate converter. Many travel models run on both systems.

Je cherche un rasoir électrique.	I am looking for an electric razor.
zheuh shersh uh ra-swar	
ay-lek-treek	

Je voudrais une crème à raser pour peau sensible.

I would like a shaving cream for sensitive skin.

zheuh voo-dray Un krem a ra-zay poor po sah-see-bl

Avez-vous un shampooing pour cheveux secs?

Do you have a shampoo for dry hair?

a-vay voo uh shah-poo-ih poor sheuh-veuh sek

 Quel salon de coiffure recommandez-vous? *(kel sa-loh deuh kwa-fUr reuh-ko-mah-day voo):* What hair salon do you recommend?

During an extended stay in France, both men and women will probably need to get their hair cut or styled. Whenever possible get a recommendation by asking *Quel salon de coiffure recommandez-vous?* (Which hair salon do you recommend?) Then tell your *coiffeur/coiffeuse* (stylist), for example: *Je veux une coupe et un brushing.* (I want a cut and blow dry.)

Je veux une coupe et un brushing.

I want a cut and blow dry.

zheuh veuh Un koop ay uh breuh-sheeng

Ne coupez pas trop court!

Don't cut it too short!

neuh koo-pay pa tro koor

Quand pouvez-vous me prendre? *(kah poo-vay voo meuh prah-dr):* When can you see me?

When you're traveling, time may be of the essence. Of course, a busy *salon de coiffure* (hair salon) will require a *rendez-vous* (appointment) with one of their *coiffeurs/coiffeuses* (stylists). Prices for various services are usually posted; however, don't hesitate to ask what a specific service will cost. Just as in the United States, a hair salon may also be a *salon de beauté* (beauty salon) with a range of services such as manicure, pedicure, and waxing.

C'est combien pour la coupe?	How much is it for the haircut?
say koh-byeh poor la koop	
Pouvez-vous me faire une manucure?	Can you do my nails?
poo-vay voo meuh fer Un ma-nU-kUr	
Pouvez-vous m'épiler les jambes?	Can you wax my legs?
poo-vay voo may-pee-lay lay zhahb	

 Il me faut un pressing. *(eel meuh fo uh pres-seeng):* I need a cleaner's.

Have you been invited to *une soirée très chic* (an elegant party)? You may want to get your suit or dress dry-cleaned (*nettoyé*[e] *à sec*) for the event. So look for *un pressing* (a dry cleaner's).

J'ai un costume à faire nettoyer.　　I have a suit to be cleaned.

zhay uh kos-tUm a fer net-wa-yay

J'ai une robe à faire nettoyer.　　I have a dress to be cleaned.

zhay Un rob a fer net-wa-yay

J'en ai besoin ce soir.　　I need it tonight.

zhah nay beuh-zwih seuh swar

 Pouvez-vous faire des retouches? *(poo-vay voo fer day reuh-toosh):* Can you make alterations?

When you buy clothing, the store will usually be happy to make *des retouches* (basic alterations); this service is often free. However, if you are in a hurry, you may be better off going to *un tailleur/une couturière* (a tailor shop) and paying for the service yourself.

La jupe est un peu longue.　　The skirt is a little long.

la zhUp ay tuh peuh lohg

Les manches sont trop longues.　　The sleeves are too long.

lay mahsh soh tro lohg

Le pantalon est un peu large.　　The pants are a little wide.

leuh pah-ta-loh ay tuh peuh larzh

Quand est-ce que ce sera prêt?　　When will it be ready?

kah tes keuh seuh seuh-ra pray

Chapter 8

Shopping for Food

 Quelle boulangerie recommandez-vous? *(kel boo-lah-zhree reuh-ko-mah-day voo)*: Which bakery do you recommend?

Are you in a mood for a *brioche*, a *croissant*, or a *pain au chocolat*? In France you can easily locate one in any town or *quartier* (neighborhood). Almost anyone you ask will be able to recommend *une excellente boulangerie*. In spite of the proliferation of *supermarchés* (supermarkets) and *hypermarchés* ("big-box" stores), which are in direct competition with independently owned bakeries, *boulangeries* are alive and well. They are everywhere, and residents become regular customers at their favorite stores.

The *boulangers* (bakers) have had to make adjustments to remain competitive in today's market. There are no limits to what you can find in a slice of "French" bread nowadays: olives, bacon, chunks of fruit or cheese, nuts, and herbs. Not to mention that your bread may also be enriched with extra calcium and other nutrients. However, despite the revival of traditional recipes for darker breads and the multitude of newly invented varieties, the basic *baguette* still represents 70 percent of French bakery sales.

The French government maintains certain controls over bread designations. A baker may call his bread *maison* only if the entire operation, from the kneading, to the baking, and to sales takes place at a single location.

 Une baguette, s'il vous plaît. *(Un ba-get seel voo play):* A baguette, please.

When you go to the *boulangerie*, ask for your *baguette*, or, if you prefer, ask for a *pain complet* (whole-wheat bread), a *pain au son* (whole wheat plus bran), or a *pain de campagne* (country-style bread); the latter will vary according to the region where it is made or where the baker is from.

Many bakeries include a *salon de thé* (tearoom) where you can help yourself to coffee and have a breakfast of *croissants au beurre* (butter croissants) or *pains au chocolat.*

un pain complet uh pih koh-play	whole-wheat bread
un pain au son uh pih o soh	whole-wheat and bran bread
un pain au seigle uh pih o se-gl	rye bread
un pain de campagne uh pih deuh kah-pa-nyeuh	country-style bread
un pain au chocolat uh pih o sho-ko-la	a chocolate croissant
un croissant au beurre uh krwa-sah o beuhr	a butter croissant

Donnez-moi un éclair au chocolat, s'il vous plaît. *(do-nay mwa euh nay-kler o sho-ko-la seel voo play):* Give me a chocolate éclair, please. ·

Many *boulangeries* are also *pâtisseries* (pastry shops); so, in addition to a range of breads, they offer a display of delicious desserts such as *tartes aux fruits* (fruit tarts), *éclairs au chocolat ou à la vanille* (chocolate or vanilla éclairs), and *gâteaux* (cakes) of all kinds including *les gâteaux d'anniversaire* (birthday cakes). Sometimes the same shop is also *un traiteur* (caterer/deli), offering a variety of lunch foods, sandwiches, salads, and delicatessen, such as *quiches*, *pâtés*, and even *charcuterie* (cold cuts), to take away. The *boulangerie-pâtisserie* can also compete with the best *confiserie* (candy shop) when it comes to creating special treats for holidays. They will bake and decorate beautiful *bûches de Noël* (Yule logs) for *Noël* (Christmas) and pastries or chocolate cakes adorned with eggs, chicks, bunnies, and bells for *Pâques* (Easter).

une tarte aux fruits	a fruit tart
uh tart o frwee	
un gâteau d'anniversaire	a birthday cake
uh ga-to da-nee-ver-ser	
un sandwich au jambon	a ham sandwich
uh sahd-weesh o zhah-boh	

 Je vais prendre une boîte de pralinés, s'il vous plaît. *(zheuh vay prah-dr Un bwat deuh pra-lee-nay seel voo play):* I'll have a box of truffles, please.

France has many *confiseries* (candy shops). They are the perfect place to get a few boxes or bags of special French candy to bring back as gifts or for personal enjoyment, that is, if sweets happen to be your

71

péché mignon (sweet sin). In addition, a *confiserie* is often a feast for the eyes as well as the palate, especially around the holidays. For instance, at *Pâques*, you will be dazzled by the creativity of the *confiseurs* and *pâtissiers* (pastry chefs) who create multitudes of hens, chicks, bunnies, and eggs, just to name a few items made from chocolate and candy.

Who has not heard of *bonbons* (literally, goody-goodys)? *Bonbons* can be *mous* (soft) or *durs* (hard); they can be *spécialités régionales* (regional specialties); they can be in the form of *chewing gum*, *caramels*, *sucettes* (lollypops), *pralinés* (truffles), etc. So be sure to buy and enjoy French candy, by *la boîte* (the box), by *la livre* (the pound), or by *le gramme* (the gram).

deux cent cinquante grammes   two hundred fifty grams of caramels
  de caramels
deuh sah sih-kaht gram deuh
  ka-ra-mel

 Est-ce que l'épicerie est encore ouverte? *(es keuh lay-pee-sree ay tah-kor oo-vert):* Is the grocery store still open?

The word *épicerie* (grocery store) comes from the word *épice* (spice). Originally a *comptoir* (counter) where one could buy spices, it became the generic name for a type of convenience store where people buy everyday items (in addition to spices). How late an *épicerie* stays open depends on whether you are in a big city or small town. These stores vary, from the simple neighborhood *épicerie* found on almost every corner of a village or town, to fancy, pricey, specialized stores such as *Hédiard*, *Fauchon*, or *La Grande Épicerie* in Paris. The local *épicerie* is where you can pick up small items like *une bouteille d'eau minérale* (a bottle of mineral water), *un paquet de petits gâteaux secs* (a package of cookies), *une boîte de biscuits salés* (a box of crackers), *une tablette de chocolat* (a chocolate bar), or *des bananes* (some bananas).

Il me faut une bouteille d'eau minérale.	I need a bottle of mineral water.
eel meuh fo Un boo-tay do mee-nay-ral	
Il me faut un paquet de petits gâteaux secs.	I need a package of cookies.
eel meuh fo uh pa-kay deuh peuh-tee ga-to sek	
Je voudrais une boîte de biscuits salés.	I would like a box of crackers.
zheuh voo-dray Un bwat deuh bees-kwee sa-lay	
Je voudrais une tablette de chocolat.	I would like a chocolate bar.
zheuh voo-dray Un ta-blet deuh sho-ko-la	

 J'aimerais un kilo de pêches. *(zhem-ray uh kee-lo deuh pesh):* I would like a kilo of peaches.

Remember to use *grammes* (grams), *livres* (pounds), and *kilos* (kilos) whenever you ask for fruit and vegetables *au marché* (at the fruit and vegetable market), or in *l'épicerie*. If a clerk is available, do not personally handle any fruit or vegetables. You may, however, ask the clerk to give you *des fruits mûrs* (ripe fruit) or *des fruits moins mûrs* (less-ripe fruit). However, supermarkets are mostly self-service; there you must select and bag your own fruit and vegetables. Often there are computerized scales on which to weigh your produce and print the price tags.

Donnez-moi environ cinq cents grammes/environ une livre de raisin, s'il vous plaît.	Please give me about five hundred grams/about a pound of grapes.
do-nay mwa ah-vee-roh sih sah gram/ah-vee-roh Un lee-vr deuh ray-sih seel voo play	
Je voudrais deux kilos de pommes.	I would like two kilos of apples.
zheuh voo-dray deuh kee-lo deuh pom	

 Quatre tranches de jambon coupées fines. *(katr trahsh deuh zah-boh koo-pay feen):* Four slices of ham thinly sliced.

A French *charcuterie* (deli) will have a great variety of cold meats such as *jambon* (zhah-boh) (ham), *saucisses* (so-sees) (sausages), *salami* (sa-la-mee) (salami), and *pâtés* (pa-tay) for sandwiches. Like produce, these products can be bought by *grammes*, *livres*, and *kilos*, or simply in *tranches* (trahsh) (slices) or *morceaux* (mor-so) (pieces). The same holds true in a *boucherie* (butcher shop) when buying meats such as *le porc* (leuh por) (pork), *le bœuf* (leuh beuhf) (beef), *l'agneau* (la-nyo) (lamb), or *le veau* (leuh vo) (veal). At the butcher shop, you may specify that you would like *un petit morceau* or *un grand morceau*. The *boucher/bouchère* will place his/her knife in various positions on the larger piece until you indicate the size you want. You can also inform him/her how many people you'll be serving by saying: *pour deux* (poor deuh) (for two) or *pour trois* (poor trwa) (for three), etc.

Un petit morceau de pâté, s'il vous plaît.	A little chunk of pâté, please.
uh peuh-tee mor-so deuh pa-tay seel voo play	
Un morceau de bœuf pour trois personnes.	A piece of beef for three people.
uh mor-so deuh beuhf poor trwa per-son	

 Fermé pour congés annuels. *(fer-may poor koh-zhay a-nU-el):* Closed for annual vacation.

If you travel in France during the summer, you'll find many small stores from *l'épicerie* to *la boulangerie*, and even *la pharmacie*, closed for summer vacation, which the French call *les grandes vacances* (the long vacation). Note that there will still be basic services available; businesses often arrange this among themselves. *Août* (August) is a favorite vacation time for the French, despite the government's effort to stagger holidays. Local businesses, such as *l'agence de voyage* (the travel agency), will also be closed on Sundays and *les jours de fête/les jours fériés* (national holidays) such as *le premier mai* (Labor Day [in France]).

**L'épicerie est fermée pour congés
 d'été au mois d'août.**
lay-pee-sree ay fer-may poor
 koh-zhay day-tay o mwa doot

The grocery store is closed for
 holidays in August.

**L'agence de voyage est fermée
 les jours fériés.**
la-zhahs deuh vwa-yazh ay fer-may
 lay zhoor fay-ryay

The travel agency closes on holidays.

 Est-ce qu'il y a un supermarché par ici? *(es keel ya uh sU-per-mar-shay par ee-see):* Is there a supermarket near here?

Supermarkets, *les supermarchés* or *les hypermarchés*, depending on their size, are often located outside urban areas near *autoroutes* (high-ways) or *routes nationales* (interstate roads). They cover huge areas where you will find just about anything from food to furniture and clothing sold *en libre-service* (self-service). Small supermarkets called *superettes* are now expanding in urban areas as well.

**Le supermarché est-il près de
 la route nationale?**
leuh sU-per-mar-shay ay teel pray
 deuh la root na-syo-nal

Is the supermarket near the
 interstate?

Est-ce que c'est un libre-service?
es keuh say tuh lee-br ser-vees

Is it self-service?

Chapter 9

Eating Out

 La carte, s'il vous plaît. *(la kart seel voo play):* The menu, please.

If you're planning to order *deux hors-d'œuvre* (two appetizers) and *un dessert* (a dessert), order your meal *à la carte*. If you're planning to order *un plat principal* (an entrée) and nothing else, again use the phrase *à la carte*. To order *à la carte*, you will need to look at the entire menu, so ask for: *La carte, s'il vous plaît.* (The menu, please.)

If, on the other hand, you wish to order an entire meal at a *prix fixe* (fixed price), a normal option in many French cafés, simply ask for *le menu du jour* (the menu of the day).

Whenever you are unsure of what a given dish is, avoid surprises by asking for an explanation: *Qu'est-ce que c'est?* (kes keuh say) (What is it?)

Le menu du jour, s'il vous plaît.	Today's menu, please.
leuh meuh-nU dU zhoor seel	
voo play	

Un café crème, s'il vous plaît. *(uh ka-fay krem seel voo play):* Coffee with cream, please.

A traditional French breakfast is a *café crème* with a *croissant* or a *baguette*, butter, and jam. A variant on the *café crème* is a *café au lait* (ka-fay o lay) (strong coffee with hot milk). A *café crème* can be ordered any time of day. If you simply order *un café*, you will get a small cup of black coffee, similar to an espresso.

Most cafés sell *croissants* (krwa-sah) in the morning, sometimes they also have *pains au chocolat* (pihn o sho-ko-la). If the café does not serve *croissants*, you may get them at the nearest bakery and bring them to your café.

 Je préfère mon steak bien cuit. *(zheuh pray-fer moh stek byeh kwee):* I prefer my steak well-done.

If you are accustomed to eating well-done beef, this phrase can save the day. The equivalent of "medium-rare" in French is *à point*. At a restaurant in France, your steak will most likely arrive cooked *saignant* (say-nyah) *ou bleu* (bleuh) (rare or very rare), unless you specify otherwise. If such is your preference, say this: *Je voudrais mon steak au poivre cuit à point* (I would like my pepper steak medium-rare) or *Je voudrais mon steak bien cuit.* (I would like my steak well-done.)

Je voudrais mon steak bien cuit.	I would like my steak well-done.
zheuh voo-dray moh stek byeh kwee	
à point	medium-rare
a pwih	
saignant	rare
say-nyah	

Je voudrais des pommes de terre vapeur. *(zheuh voo-dray day pom deuh ter va-peuhr):* I would like steamed potatoes.

You may find that vegetables in French restaurants are often more cooked and less crisp than you expect. However, before you decide to make a special request, such as to prepare a dish differently, or to put certain ingredients on the side, as is often acceptable in the United States, note that individual French chefs are very proud of their unique cuisine and will refuse to change their *recettes* (recipes) according to customers' requests. Similarly, diners very rarely would ask a waiter to substitute one side dish for another.

Many meat and fish dishes cooked in sauces come with *pommes de terre à la vapeur* (steamed potatoes). The main food in a compound phrase such as *œuf à la coque* is always the first word, in this case the egg, while the following phrase, such as *à la coque* (in the shell or soft-boiled), identifies the way it's cooked. (A hard-boiled egg is *un œuf dur.*) Often the second phrase identifies a main ingredient in the dish; for example, *une omelette aux champignons* is an omelet with mushrooms, *un sandwich au jambon* is a ham sandwich, and *un chou à la crème* is a cream-filled pastry. In *la glace au chocolat*, the second noun tells you the flavor of the ice cream; in *une crêpe au Grand Marnier*, the *Grand Marnier* is the liquor added to the *crêpe.*

Je désire un œuf à la coque.	I want a soft-boiled egg.
zheuh voo-dray euh neuhf a la kok	
Je voudrais une omelette aux champignons.	I would like a mushroom omelet.
zheuh voo-dray Un om-let o shah-pee-nyoh	

Je voudrais un sandwich au jambon.	I would like a ham sandwich.
zheuh voo-dray uh sahnd-weesh o zhah-boh	
Je voudrais une glace au chocolat.	I would like a chocolate ice cream.
zheuh voo-dray Un glas o sho-ko-la	
Je voudrais une crêpe au Grand Marnier.	I would like a Grand Marnier crêpe.
zheuh voo-dray Un krep o grah mar-nyay	
Je voudrais un chou à la crème.	I would like a cream puff.
zheuh voo-dray uh shoo a la krem	

 Qu'est-ce que c'est comme sauce? *(kes-keuh say kom sos):* What kind of sauce is it?

French cuisine is well known for its rich variety of sauces such as *sauce blanche* (white sauce), *sauce brune* (brown sauce), *rouille* (spicy sauce), or *coulis* (sweet or savory sauce). Many sauces are made with wine: *sauce bourguignonne* (sauce made with Burgundy), while others, such as *sauce hollandaise*, have a butter base. If you are not familiar with a certain sauce, ask your server to explain how it is made by asking the questions: *Comment c'est fait?* (kom-mah say fay) (How's it made?) or *En quoi ça consiste?* (ah kwa sa koh-seest) (What's it made of?)

If you prefer to avoid eating meals made with rich sauces, seek out restaurants that specialize in lighter fare, *la nouvelle cuisine.*

Comment c'est fait, une sauce blanche?	How is a white sauce made?
kom-mah say fay Un sos blahsh	

Comment c'est fait, une sauce brune?	How is a brown sauce made?
kom-mah say fay Un sos brUn	
Comment c'est fait, une sauce bourguignonne?	How is a Burgundy sauce made?
kom-mah say fay Un sos boor-gee-nyon	
Comment c'est fait, une sauce hollandaise?	How is a Hollandaise sauce made?
kom-mah say fay Un sos o-lah-dez	

 Je prends le poulet Provençal. *(zheuh prah leuh poo-lay pro-vah-sal):* I'll have the chicken Provençal.

Some French dishes have names that include the adjective *Provençal*, derived from the name of the *Provence* region, inland from the French Riviera (which the French call *la Côte d'Azur*). These dishes usually contain Mediterranean ingredients such as *huile d'olive* (olive oil), *tomates* (tomatoes), *ail* (garlic), and the famous *herbes de Provence* (a mixture of rosemary, thyme, marjoram, basil, bay leaves, and lavender). Dishes are often named for the region or the city where they were first made and remain a specialty, such as: *bœuf bourguignonne* (beef in Burgundy wine), *choucroute alsacienne* (Alsatian sauerkraut), *salade niçoise* (Nice-style salad), or *crêpes normandes* (Normandy-style crêpes). If the menu does not show the ingredients in a dish, use these phrases: *Qu'est-ce que c'est?* (kes-keuh say) (What is it?) or *Qu'est-ce qu'il y a dans… ?* (kes keel ya dah) (What is in . . . ?) before you order.

Je prends la choucroute alsacienne.	I'll have the Alsatian sauerkraut.
zheuh prah la shoo-kroot al-za-syen	

Je prends la quiche lorraine. — I'll have the quiche Lorraine.

zheuh prah la keesh lo-ren

Je prends le bœuf bourguignonne. — I'll have the Burgundy beef.

zheuh prah leuh beuhf

   boor-gee-nyoh

Je prends l'agneau breton. — I'll have the Breton-style lamb

zheuh prah la-nyo breuh-toh   (from Brittany).

Qu'est-ce qu'il y a dans la — What is in the *crêpe normande*

   crêpe normande?   (Normandy style)?

kes-keel ya dah la krep nor-mahd

Qu'est-ce qu'il y a dans la salade — What is in the *salade niçoise* (Nice

   niçoise?   style)?

kes-keel ya dah la sa-lad nee-swaz

 Je suis allergique à... *(zheuh swee za-ler-zheek a):* I am allergic to . . .

Many people are prone to food allergies, and those who don't have them are aware of them. Nothing is worse than a vacation or a business trip ruined by an allergic reaction to a food. To prevent this from happening, memorize the following phrases, if they apply, or modify them according to your own needs. Don't forget to use them before ordering any meal.

Je suis allergique aux fruits de mer. — I am allergic to seafood.

zheuh swee za-ler-zheek o frwee

   deuh mer

Je suis allergique aux cacahuètes. — I am allergic to peanuts.

zheuh swee za-ler-zheek o ka-ka-wet

Je suis allergique aux produits laitiers.

zheuh swee za-ler-zheek o pro-dwee lay-tyay

I am allergic to dairy products.

Je suis allergique aux œufs.

zheuh swee za-ler-zheek o zeuhf

I am allergic to eggs.

 Qu'est-ce que vous recommandez comme vin? *(kes-keuh voo reuh-kom-mah-day kom vih)*: What wine do you recommend?

Feel free to ask this question if you are not particularly a wine connoisseur but like to taste different wines. You can also ask your waiter to recommend, for example, a light red wine: *Qu'est-ce que vous recommandez comme vin rouge léger?* (kes keuh voo reuh-kom-mah-day kom vih roozh lay-zhay) or a sweet white wine: *Qu'est-ce que vous recommandez comme vin blanc doux?* (kes keuh voo reuh-kom-mah-day kom vih blah doo). Since the French often have *un apéritif* (a predinner drink) before the meal and/or *un digestif* (usually a liqueur) after the meal, feel free to tweak the phrase accordingly.

Qu'est-ce que vous recommandez comme apéritifs?

kes-keuh voo reuh-kom-mah-day kom a-pay-ree-teef

What *apéritifs* do you recommend?

Qu'est-ce que vous recommandez comme digestifs?

kes-keuh voo reuh-kom-mah-day kom dee-zhes-teef

What after-dinner drinks do you recommend?

Qu'est-ce que vous recommandez   What appetizers do you recommend?
   comme hors-d'œuvre?
kes-keuh voo reuh-kom-mah-day
   kom or-deuhvr

Qu'est-ce que vous recommandez   What desserts do you recommend?
   comme desserts?
kes-keuh voo reuh-kom-mah-day
   kom des-ser

 Pas trop salé, s'il vous plaît. *(pa tro sa-lay seel voo play)*:
Not too salty, please.

Although it is generally not a good idea to ask for items "on the side" or for substitutions to the ingredients in your dish (the chef might feel that his art is less than appreciated), your individual diet may require that you have, for example, *la vinaigrette à part* (salad dressing on the side). It is also reasonable to request that your dish be *pas trop salé* (not too salty). If you are accustomed to vegetables *al dente* (crispy) as they often are in the U.S., you may not enjoy the traditionally well-cooked *haricots verts* (green beans) or *carottes* (carrots) served to you. It might be worth requesting that they be *pas trop cuits* (not too cooked).

Pas trop cuit, s'il vous plaît.   Not too well-done, please.
pa tro kwee seel voo play

Pas de vinaigrette, s'il vous plaît.   No dressing, please.
pa deuh vee-nay-gret seel voo play

La vinaigrette à part, s'il vous plaît.   The dressing on the side, please.
la vee-nay-gret a par seel voo play

Je crois que c'est une erreur. *(zheuh krwa keuh say tUn er-reuhr)*: I think this is a mistake.

When everything goes well, dining out is a wonderful experience, but mistakes can happen even in the best restaurants. Should you be the victim of a mishap, for example, getting the wrong dish, use this phrase to correct the situation. If the server does not understand, tell him/her: *Je n'ai pas commandé cela.* (I did not order this.) Remember that French servers are professionals and deserve to be treated with respect. Always use the traditional *monsieur/madame/mademoiselle* (sir/madam/miss) and a phrase such as *Excusez-moi* (Excuse me).

Je n'ai pas commandé cela.   I did not order this.

zheuh nay pa kom-mah-day seuh-la

 Monsieur/Mademoiselle, l'addition, s'il vous plaît!
(meuh-syeuh/mad-mwa-zel la-dee-syoh seel voo play): Sir/Miss, the check, please!

The method of delivering the bill varies with the café or restaurant. In very busy cafés, you may be expected to pay as soon as your order is delivered to you: *un reçu* (uh reuh-sU) (a cash register receipt) may be left on your table with your order. When you pay, the waiter partially tears the receipt to show you have paid. In other restaurants, when you finish your meal, you will ask your server for the bill when you are ready to leave.

To get the attention of the server, be sure to call him or her *Monsieur*, *Mademoiselle*, or *Madame*, and use *s'il vous plaît*.

After a meal, you may linger at your table, nursing that *digestif* or coffee, whether you are alone or with friends. The French do not like to be rushed when they are eating out; that explains why your bill may take a long time to come, that is, if you haven't requested it with one of these customary expressions: *L'addition, s'il vous plaît/La note, s'il vous plaît* (Check, please) or *Je vous dois combien?* (How much do I owe you?) Do not ask if *le service est compris* (leuh ser-vees ay koh-pree) (service is included), since French cafés and restaurants will automatically include it in the bill. You may, however, leave an extra *pourboire* (tip), usually a few coins, if the service was especially good or if you hope to become *un habitué/une habituée* (a regular) of the establishment. If you happen to receive the wrong bill, bring it to the attention of the server by saying: *Ce n'est pas mon addition.* (This is not my bill.)

La note, s'il vous plaît!   Check, please!
la not seel voo play

Je vous dois combien?   How much do I owe you?
zheuh voo dwa koh-byeh

Ce n'est pas mon addition.   This is not my check.
seuh nay pa mo na-dee-syoh

 Les toilettes, s'il vous plaît. *(lay twa-let seel voo play):* The restroom, please.

Restrooms in cafés are not for the public, but only for customers. It is considered very rude to go into a café only to use the restroom. If you need to make a restroom stop, enter a café and order something; then use the restroom while your order is being prepared. Do not ask for *une salle de bains* as this describes a bathroom complete with shower and tub.

Most towns have *les toilettes publiques* (public bathrooms), usually near parking lots or tourist information offices. You may use those, sometimes for a small fee.

Chapter 10

Entertainment

 Où joue-t-on un bon film? *(oo zhoo-toh uh boh feelm)*:
Where's there a good movie playing?

France offers a multitude of types of entertainment for locals as well as tourists. Whether you love cinema, theater, concerts, or dance, you'll have a tremendous amount to choose from.

Paris especially is known as a paradise for lovers of cinema. The city has hundreds of movie theaters where both French and international movies from all eras of cinema are shown. After all, the French have bestowed the term *le septième art* (the seventh art) to cinema. Going out to a movie remains a favorite Parisian *passe-temps*. Some *salles de cinéma* (movie theaters), such as the *Grand Rex*, are huge. Others, like the *Géode* with its hemispheric screens, are the epitome of advanced technology. And you can still go to screening rooms with a tiny number of seats. The *Champs-Élysées*, the *Opéra* district (especially the *boulevard des Italiens*), and the *Quartier Latin* are the Parisian meccas of cinema. For detailed programs, get a copy of the weekly Paris magazines *Pariscope* or *L'Officiel des Spectacles*, which come out each Wednesday. Note that films dubbed into French are labeled "VF";

if they are shown in English, it will say *version anglaise*; if in the original language, with French subtitles, it will say "VO" for *version originale*. For these, be prepared to read the French subtitles. If you have a spur of the moment desire to see a movie, ask a desk clerk at your hotel: *Où joue-t-on un bon film?* or *Où passe-t-on un bon film?*

À quelle heure est la séance de cinéma?

At what time does the show start?

a kel euhr ay la say-ahs deuh see-nay-ma

 Où est-ce qu'il y a une bonne disco(thèque)? *(oo es keel ya Un bon dees-ko [-tek]):* Where is there a good disco(theque)?

If you want to spend an evening *à la disco* (at a disco) or *dans une boîte de nuit* (at a nightclub), make sure to check the minimum age requirement. In France it is usually sixteen.

Quel est l'âge minimum dans cette discothèque?

What is the minimum age in this discotheque?

kel ay lazh mee-nee-meuhm dah set dees-ko-tek

 Qu'est-ce qui joue au théâtre en ce moment? *(kes kee zhoo o tay-a-tr ah seuh mo-mah):* What is playing at the theater these days?

The most famous Paris theater is the *Comédie Française*, founded in the seventeenth century under Louis XIV, *le roi soleil* (the Sun King), to showcase Molière's comedies. The *Comédie Française* is also the national theater of France and has branches in every sizable French city. It specializes in (but is not restricted to) classical plays. Many other theaters put on typically French *théâtre de boulevard* shows, still others focus on experimental theater. It is easy to find a wide variety of plays, dance, and music programs from all over the world. Seek the advice of your friends or your concierge by asking them what is currently playing: *Qu'est-ce qui joue au théâtre en ce moment?*, or tell them what you generally like by using one of the questions below:

Où est-ce que je peux voir une pièce de théâtre classique?	Where can I see a classical play?
oo es keuh zheuh peuh vwar Un pyes deuh tay-a-tr kla-seek	
Où est-ce qu'il y a des concerts gratuits?	Where can I see a free concert?
oo es keel ya day koh-ser gra-twee	

 Est-ce qu'il y a encore des tickets/des billets pour le concert ce soir? *(es keel ya ah-kor day tee-kay/day bee-yay poor leuh koh-ser seuh swar):* Are there still tickets for tonight's concert?

Classical music lovers will be enthralled by the great variety of offerings in major French cities. In Paris, of course, you shouldn't miss the opportunity to hear music in some of the city's *grands théâtres*. Whether you go to the sumptuous *Opéra Garnier* or the contemporary *Opéra Bastille*, you will always remember the experience. Built between 1862 and 1875 by Charles Garnier, the *Opéra Garnier* has a baroque façade, monumental stairs, and an Italian-style hall with ceiling paintings by twentieth-century artist Marc Chagall. Since the opening of the *Opéra Bastille* in 1989, the *Opéra Garnier* is used as a ballet theater. On a different scale, there are also *les concerts de jour*

(lunchtime concerts) in churches, *la musique médiévale* (medieval music), and *les chorales* (choirs) at the *Sainte-Chapelle* on *l'Île de la Cité* as well as *la musique de chambre* (chamber music) at the *Orangerie*.

J'aimerais une place au balcon.　I would like a balcony seat.
zhem-ray Un plas o bal-koh
Où est-ce qu'on joue de la　Where do they play chamber music?
　musique de chambre?
oo es koh zhoo deuh la mU-zeek
　deuh shah-br

 Sur quelle chaîne peut-on voir CNN? *(sUr kel shen peuh-toh vwar say-en-en):* On what channel can we see CNN?

What is available for viewing on television in French hotels will depend on the hotel. You will most likely have access to a few French-language public broadcasting channels and some private channels, as well as channels from neighboring countries.

Avez-vous un programme télé?　Do you have a TV guide?
a-vay voo uh pro-gram tay-lay
Est-ce que je peux commander　May I order a movie?
　un film?
es keuh zheuh peuh ko-mah-day
　uh feelm

Où est-ce qu'il y a un spectacle Son et Lumière? *(oo es keel ya uh spek-ta-kl soh ay lU-myer):* Where is there a Sound and Light show?

A *Son et Lumière* is a sound and light show which usually takes place in a historic setting and always at night. Special lighting effects are projected onto the façade of a building or ruin and synchronized with recorded or live narration and music to dramatize the history of the place. If you travel through the Loire Valley, you will surely have opportunities to see one of those shows in the setting of a *château* (castle).

Est-ce qu'il y a un Son et Lumière en anglais? es keel ya uh soh ay lU-myer ah nah-glay	Is there a sound and light show in English?
Quel est le thème du spectacle? kel ay leuh tem dU spek-ta-kl	What is the theme of the show?

 Vous pouvez me faire une réservation pour deux au Moulin Rouge? *(voo poo-vay meuh fer Un ray-zer-va-syoh poor deuh o moo-lih roozh):* Can you make me a reservation for two at the Moulin Rouge?

The legendary Parisian cabaret famous for its French cancan was first immortalized by the late-nineteenth-century French painter Toulouse-Lautrec and has more recently been brought back to fame in the Hollywood musical *Moulin Rouge*. Its stage has seen numerous French stars such as Édith Piaf and international stars such as Frank Sinatra. You can enjoy a dinner show with champagne in a *belle époque* décor in this historic place. Some Parisian cabarets now include limousine transportation in the price of the dinner show, useful after a long evening. So don't hesitate to inquire as to what exactly is included in the price of a show.

Est-ce que le prix du dîner est compris?	Is the price of dinner included?
es keuh leuh pree dU dee-nay ay koh-pree	
Est-ce qu'il y a un tarif minimum?	Is there a minimum charge?
es keel ya uh ta-reef mee-nee-mum	
Est-ce que le prix comprend le transport?	Does the price include transportation?
es keuh leuh pree koh-prah leuh trahs-por	

 Où est-ce qu'on peut trouver un bon club de jazz? *(oo es koh peuh troo-vay uh boh kleuhb deuh zhaz):* Where can we find a good jazz club?

France and especially Paris have been home to jazz and jazz musicians almost since the beginnings of this musical genre. It should be easy for jazz lovers to find good clubs and jazz performances. In addition, from late spring to the end of September, music festivals, including jazz fests, are held just about everywhere in France.

Est-ce qu'il y a un concert de jazz quelque part?	Is there a jazz concert somewhere?
es keel ya uh koh-ser deuh zhaz kel-keuh par	

Chapter 11

Museums to Mountains

 Adressez-vous au syndicat d'initiative. *(a-dres-say voo o sih-dee-ka dee-nee-sya-teev)*: Inquire at the tourist office.

You might hear this advice from the hotel concierge if your question is beyond his/her knowledge. Note that this phrase could be easily misinterpreted if taken literally. Here, the word *initiative* refers to local tourist projects, and *le syndicat* is the office that manages information to help and guide tourists. You'll find brochures, flyers, maps, and information on hotels, restaurants, tourist sites, festivals, and shows. You can also book *des tours* (guided tours) and secure *le transport* (transportation) at a *syndicat*. There are several in every region; every major city and many towns have them. So when you plan your itinerary, visit the website of the *syndicats* in the regions or cities you plan to visit, or if you prefer to do things spontaneously, visit one *sur place* (on the spot).

Je cherche un guide.	I am looking for a guide (person
zheuh shersh uh geed	or book).

Je voudrais un renseignement.   I would like some information.
zheuh voo-dray uh rah-se-nyeuh-mah

Avez-vous une brochure/un   Do you have a brochure/a flyer?
  prospectus?
a-vay voo Un bro-shUr/uh
  pros-pek-tUs

J'ai besoin d'un plan.   I need a (city/site) map.
zhay beuh-zwih duh plah

 Pourriez-vous m'indiquer... ? *(poo-ryay voo mih-dee-kay):* Could you point out . . . ?

Are you looking for the Louvre metro station? Use one of the previously mentioned lead-in phrases such as *Pardon/Excusez-moi, Madame*, and follow up with this extremely polite and useful phrase: *Pourriez-vous m'indiquer le métro du Louvre?* (Could you point out the Louvre metro station?) Or, alternatively, ask: *Pourriez-vous me dire où est le métro du Louvre?* (Could you tell me where the Louvre metro station is?)

If you cannot remember either of these rather long questions, simply ask where the Louvre metro station is: *Où est le métro du Louvre?* or *Où se trouve le métro du Louvre?*, and hope that your respondent does not mind this more direct approach.

Finally, if you've lost your way walking to the Louvre museum and want to show a passerby that you really do know and understand some French, ask him/her: *Quel est le chemin pour le musée du Louvre?* (Which way to the Louvre museum?) or *Est-ce que c'est à droite ou à gauche? Est-ce que c'est tout droit?* (Is it to the left or to the right? Is it straight ahead?)

Pourriez-vous me dire où est le métro du Louvre?	Could you tell me where the Louvre subway station is?
poo-ryay voo meuh deer oo ay leuh may-tro dU loo-vr	
Où se trouve le métro?	Where is the subway?
oo seuh troov leuh may-tro	
Pourriez-vous me dire où se trouve...?	Could you tell me where is . . . ?
poo-ryay voo meuh deer oo seuh troov	
Quel est le chemin pour... ?	Which way is it to . . . ?
kel ay leuh sheuh-mih poor	
Est-ce que c'est à gauche ou à droite?	Is it to the right or to the left?
es keuh say ta gosh oo a drwat	
Est-ce que c'est tout droit?	Is it straight ahead?
es keuh say too drwa	

 J'ai entendu parler d'une église médiévale. *(zhay ah-tah-dU par-lay dUn ay-gleez may-dyay-val):* I heard about a medieval church.

The phrase *J'ai entendu parler de* can prove very handy. If you heard about *une exposition d'art* (an art exhibit), *un concert*, *un spectacle* (a show), *une cathédrale, une église* (a church), *une synagogue*, or *un château*, use this expression when you're talking to your hotel concierge or the agent at a *syndicat d'initiative* to get more information regarding *où et quand* (where and when). For example: *J'ai entendu parler d'un concert dans une église à Saint-Germain.* (zhay ah-tah-dU par-lay duh kon-ser dah zU nay-gleez a sih zher-mih) (I heard about a concert in a church in Saint-Germain.) *Pouvez-vous me dire où et quand il aura*

lieu? (poo-vay voo meuh deer oo ay kah eel o-ra lyeuh) (Can you tell me where and when it will take place?)

If you want to verify that something you heard is true, use a slightly modified version of the previous phrase. For instance, tell your concierge or the agent: *J'ai entendu dire que les musées nationaux sont fermés le mardi. Est-ce vrai?* (zhay ah-tah-dU deer keuh lay mU-zay na-syo-no soh fer-may leuh mar-dee es vray) (I heard that the national museums are closed on Tuesdays. Is it true?)

J'ai entendu dire que les musées	I heard that national museums are
nationaux sont fermés le mardi.	closed on Tuesdays.
zhay ah-tah-dU deer keuh lay	
mU-zay na-syo-no soh fer-may	
leuh mar-dee	

✈ **Une carte musée, s'il vous plaît.** *(Un kart mU-zay seel voo play):* A museum access card, please.

Renaissance poet Joachim Du Bellay wrote this now famous line in one of his poems: *France, mère des arts, des armes et des lois* (France, mother of arts, arms, and laws). The French government is proud of its plethora of museums, galleries, and salons devoted to virtually any topic imaginable. The French themselves are proud of *le patrimoine français* (the French cultural and artistic heritage) and enjoy spending many of their weekends in museums. Therefore, to avoid the crowds, it's a good idea for tourists to schedule their visits on a weekday. In Paris, one can avoid *les queues* (the lines) by purchasing a *carte musée* in advance from the Paris Tourist Office, with branches at every railroad station as well as at the Eiffel Tower. This card grants unlimited visits and priority access to sixty-five locations in and around the City of Light.

 J'ai une carte d'étudiant. *(zhay Un kart day-tU-dyah):* I have a student ID.

If you have a student or educator ID, you will save money wherever you go sightseeing. Just say: *J'ai une carte d'étudiant/de professeur* (zhay Un kart day-tU-dyah/deuh pro-fes-seuhr) and show it with your passport; this will often give you a *tarif réduit* (reduced rate) or an *entrée libre* (free admission). Otherwise you will pay *plein tarif* (full price).

All visitors get free admission to a *musée national* on the first Sunday of each month, on Museum Night in May, and during the celebration of the French *patrimoine* each year on the third weekend of September. Elsewhere, young people under eighteen, teachers, senior citizens, and journalists often get in free or at a reduced price as long as they can show the appropriate *justificatif* (document).

J'ai une carte d'étudiant.	I have a student ID.
zhay Un kart day-tU-dyah	
J'ai une carte de professeur.	I have a teacher ID.
zhay Un kart deuh pro-fes-seuhr	
Il y a des tarifs réduits?	Are there reduced rates?
eel ya day ta-reef ray-dwee	
Il faut payer plein tarif?	Do we have to pay full price?
eel fo pay-yay plih ta-reef	
L'entrée est libre?	Is the admission free?
lah-tray ay lee-br	

Veuillez laisser vos effets au vestiaire. *(veuh-yay les-say vo zay-fay o ves-tyer):* Please leave your things in the coatroom.

Many large museums have *un vestiaire* (a coatroom) where you may leave your belongings. This is usually a free service to people with entrance tickets, and visitors are encouraged to do so. Look for the notice *Prière de laisser vos effets au vestiaire.* (Please leave your things in the coatroom.) Other notices may tell you *Prière de suivre le guide* (Please follow the guide) and *Prière de vous adresser au bureau d'accueil.* (Please go to the reception desk.)

Veuillez suivre le guide.
Please follow the guide.
veuh-yay swee-vr leuh geed

Adressez-vous au bureau
Go to the reception desk.
   d'accueil.
a-dres-say voo o bU-ro da-keuhy

 Un fauteuil roulant est-il disponible? *(uh fo-teuhy roo-lah ay teel dees-po-nee-bl):* Is a wheelchair available?

To accommodate a visitor who has difficulty walking, ask: *Un fauteuil roulant est-il disponible?* (Is a wheelchair available?) If you require a child's stroller, ask for *une poussette* (Un poo-set) (a stroller) the same way: *Une poussette est-elle disponible?* (Un poo-set ay tel dees-po-nee-bl).

Un audioguide est-il disponible?
Is an audioguide available?
euh no-dyo-geed ay teel
   dees-po-nee-bl

Des écouteurs sont-ils disponibles?
day zay-koo-teuhr soh teel dees-po-nee-bl

Are earphones available?

 Où est le point de départ des croisières sur la Seine? *(oo ay leuh pwih deuh day-par day krwa-zyer sUr la sen):* Where is the departure point for cruises on the Seine?

Cruising on the Seine day or night is a popular tourist activity in Paris. There are several companies that offer these cruises on riverboats called *bateaux-mouches* (literally, [house]fly-boat). These often have an open upper deck and an enclosed lower deck. The approximately hour-long tours usually include multilingual live or recorded commentary about the sights along the river. Both *la Rive gauche* (the Left Bank) and *la Rive droite* (the Right Bank) are visible from the boat. Among many other sights, you can see the *musée d'Orsay*, the Louvre museum, the Eiffel Tower, Notre-Dame Cathedral, and a number of beautiful bridges. Some companies offer lunch and dinner cruises as well.

Les bateaux-mouches partent du pont de l'Alma.
lay ba-to moosh part dU poh deuh lal-ma

The riverboats depart from the Alma bridge.

Est-ce que le dîner est inclus dans le prix?
es keuh leuh dee-nay ay tih-klU dah leuh pree

Is dinner included in the price?

Combien de temps dure le tour?
koh-byeh deuh tah dUr leuh toor

How long is the tour?

Est-ce que le terrain de camping a une plage? *(es keuh leuh ter-rih deuh kah-peeng a Un plash):* Does the campground have a beach?

For tourists eager to experience camping French style, there are approximately 11,000 *terrains de camping* (campgrounds) in France. If you want to camp, you may want to rent an RV or perhaps a tent and other gear for car-camping, but you won't have any trouble locating a campground that suits your taste and style. Various websites allow you to search by region, by number of stars (showing availability of nearby hotels and restaurants), by types of amenities, etc. Your search may yield results such as *un terrain de camping à trois étoiles* (a three-star campground) or *un terrain avec une plage* (a campground with a beach). A more detailed search will tell you: *L'équipement comprend des douches chaudes.* (The amenities include hot showers.) Of course, any *syndicat d'initiative* will be able to help you to find a campground that is appropriate for you.

Est-ce que c'est un terrain à trois étoiles?
Is it a three-star campground?
es keuh say tuh ter-rih a trwa zay-twal

Est-ce qu'il y a des douches chaudes?
Are there hot showers?
es keel ya day doosh shod

L'équipement comprend des douches chaudes.
The amenities include hot showers.
lay-keep-mah koh-prah day doosh shod

Je voudrais faire une randonnée en montagne. *(zheuh voo-dray fer Un rah-don-nay ah moh-ta-nyeuh):* I would like to take a hike in the mountains.

If you find you're able to plan an additional few days or weeks in France, use the above phrase at the *syndicat* or travel agency. There are enough mountain ranges in France for any visitor to find just the right scenery and the right activities to suit his/her style. Whether it is renting a Swiss-style chalet in the Alps and participating in winter sports, wandering through the *collines corses* (Corsican hills), hiking in the *Pyrénées* or the *Massif Central*, discovering the *vallées* (valleys), *lacs* (lakes), and *forêts* (forests) of the Vosges mountains, you will undoubtedly enjoy the calm and harmony of the landscape.

France has an extremely long coastline (3,427 km) dotted with world-class beaches. They vary from one coastal area to another. Most of them are soft, clean, and sandy, offering excellent conditions for sunbathing and other recreation, including a range of exciting water sports.

The French Mediterranean coast south of Provence (known as the French Riviera by North Americans, but *la Côte d'Azur* by Europeans) is famous for its beautiful beaches covered with *galets* (smooth rocks) and its trendy vacation spots such as Nice, Antibes, Cannes, and St-Tropez, not to mention the principality of Monaco. The northern part of the Atlantic coast features fishing villages turned resort towns such as Deauville, St-Malo, and La Rochelle, in addition to *Mont St-Michel*, called one of the Seven Wonders of the World, and the historic beaches where the Allied Forces landed on D-Day in June 1944. The beaches bordering the Atlantic are sandy, but the water tends to be cold and rough, excellent for surfing, however. The southern part of the Atlantic coast features vineyards and the city of Bordeaux.

Je veux faire un tour de la vallée de la Loire.	I want to go on a tour of the Loire Valley.
zheuh veuh fer uh toor deuh la va-lay deuh la lwar	
Est-ce qu'il y a une excursion sur les plages de Normandie?	Is there a trip to the Normandy beaches?
es keel ya Un eks-kUr-syoh sUr lay plazh deuh nor-mah-dee	
Je veux faire une réservation pour le tour de Monaco.	I want to make a reservation for the Monaco tour.
zheuh veuh fer Un ray-zer-va-syoh poor le toor deuh mo-na-ko	

 Où est-ce qu'on peut faire du cyclisme? *(oo es koh peuh fer dU see-klees-meuh):* Where can we go bicycling?

When it comes to spending leisure time in France, the choices and opportunities are endless. You can go diving in the Mediterranean, cycling through the countryside, horseback riding in the Mediter-ranean Camargue region; you can take a vacation cruise on the Seine toward the Atlantic, or fly over the Loire valley in a hot air balloon.

Où est-ce qu'on peut faire de la plongée?	Where can we go diving?
oo es koh peuh fer deuh la ploh-zhay	
Où est-ce qu'on peut faire de l'escalade?	Where can we go mountain climbing?
oo es koh peuh fer deuh les-ka-lad	

**Où est-ce qu'on peut faire
des randonnées?**
oo es koh peuh fer day rah-don-nay

Where can we go for hikes?

**Où est-ce qu'on peut faire
de l'équitation?**
oo es koh peuh fer deuh
lay-kee-ta-syoh

Where can we go horseback riding?

Chapter 12

Common Warnings

 Attention! *(a-tah-syoh):* Attention! Watch out!

Several warning expressions in French include the word *Attention!* This word will be translated differently according to context. As you are about to cross a busy street you could hear: *Attention! Vous allez vous faire écraser!* (Watch out! You're going to get yourself run over!)

Aboard a plane, when you hear the announcement: *Nous vous demandons votre attention*, you are being asked to pay attention. In a train station, the announcement *Attention au départ!* is your warning to get ready for the departure of this train.

As you enter busy tourist areas and sites such as Notre-Dame Cathedral in Paris, you may notice a sign bearing the warning *Attention aux pickpockets!* As you step off a bus or a taxi, a considerate driver may warn you to watch your step by saying: *Attention à la marche!* On the road, if you see the sign: *Attention aux travaux*, watch out for road construction or repair work.

Attention au départ!	Ready for departure!
at-tah-syoh o day-par	
Attention aux pickpockets!	Watch for pickpockets!
at-tah-syoh o peek-po-kay	
Attention à la marche!	Watch the step!
at-tah-syoh a la marsh	
Attention aux travaux.	Watch out for construction.
at-tah-syoh o tra-vo	

 Ne pas fumer. *(neuh pa fU-may):* No smoking.

Now that France has additional laws against smoking in many public places, the signs *Ne pas fumer* or *Interdit de fumer* are far more prevalent. At museums or art exhibits, signs bearing the phrase *Ne pas toucher* warn you not to touch items displayed.

The sign *Propriété privée* is often accompanied by the phrase *Défense d'entrer sous peine d'amende.* It warns you that this is private property and that you will be fined for trespassing. Similarly, the sign *Défense de marcher sur le gazon* (Don't step on the grass) should be taken seriously.

Ne pas toucher.	Do not touch.
neuh pa too-shay	
Interdit de fumer.	Smoking is forbidden.
ih-ter-dee deuh fU-may	
Défense d'entrer.	Do not enter.
day-fahs dah-tray	

Pas de photos, s'il vous plaît! *(pa deuh fo-to seel voo play):* No photos, please!

To enjoy your museum visit and avoid confrontations, inform yourself of *le règlement* (the rules). These are usually available in brochures, with additional reminders on signs. For example, at the Louvre museum, photography for private use is allowed only in rooms that showcase *les collections permanentes* (permanent collections). Flash photography is prohibited. If, dazzled by what you see, you get carried away and forget the rules, you will most likely be reminded by a guard with a warning such as: *Pas de photos* or *Pas de flash, s'il vous plaît!* (No photos *or* No flash, please!)

In rooms or galleries devoted to *les expositions temporaires* (temporary exhibits), photography and filming are strictly forbidden.

 Il est formellement interdit de marcher sur le gazon. *(eel ay for-mel-mah ih-ter-dee deuh mar-shay sUr leuh ga-zoh):* It is strictly forbidden to step on the grass.

France is a nation of *lois* (laws). This may explain why so many of them are regularly broken. The French parliament passes approximately seventy new laws each year. Many of them aim at protecting society's disadvantaged or vulnerable people. For example, a rental property owner may not evict a *locataire* (tenant) during the winter months (November to March). This type of law is *rigoureusement* (rigorously) enforced.

Other laws that are *formellement* (firmly) enforced were passed to protect public sites such as parks, *les jardins de fleurs* (flower gardens), and *les pelouses* or *le gazon* (lawns). If you read the words *pelouse* or *gazon* on a sign, it is a clue that this is not an area that you may step or sit on. There is a clear distinction between *l'herbe* (the generic word for "grass") and *le gazon* or *la pelouse*, which are usually well-maintained and manicured grassy areas. Tourist spots like the Eiffel Tower and many museums and castles such as Versailles and those in the Loire Valley are surrounded by *jardins* (gardens) and *pelouses* (lawns). Security guards will approach or call out to you if you attempt to take a short cut or have a picnic on the grass. On signs, be especially mindful of words such as *formellement* or *rigoureusement*. These are warnings that failure to abide by the rules may mean *une amende* (a fine).

 Silence, s'il vous plaît! *(see-lahs seel voo play)*: Silence, please!

This is a warning you might get in a movie theater when the movie is about to start. The French government recently approved the use of cell phone jamming equipment in cinemas, concert halls, and theaters. However, the legislation also requires that jamming devices allow emergency calls to be made.

In addition, the phrase *Silence, s'il vous plaît* is every schoolteacher's perennial warning to students to quiet down. A rather more direct and personal way to ask for silence would be: *Taisez-vous, s'il vous plaît.* (Please be quiet.)

Chapter 13

Emergencies

 Où est la gendarmerie la plus proche? *(oo ay la zhah-dar-mree la plU prosh):* Where is the closest *gendarmerie*?

The *gendarmes* (somewhat like the U.S. National Guard) are military personnel working under the French Ministry of Defense for military missions and under supervision of the Ministry of the Interior for police work. They deal mainly with keeping order outside urban areas, but perform other functions such as military rescue missions. Their headquarters are called *gendarmeries*. In urban areas you will more likely find *les commissariats de police* (police stations) staffed by *les agents de police* (police officers). *Les commissariats* are headquarters for the national police force.

 On m'a volé ma voiture! *(oh ma vo-lay ma vwa-tUr):* My car was stolen!

Since *les systèmes anti-vols* (antitheft devices) on new cars are more and more secure, cars targeted for theft are often at least ten years old and are not equipped with devices such as *les clés codées* (coded keys). Thus, chances are slim that your rental car would be stolen. Your car might, however, be *vandalisée* (vah-da-lee-zay) (vandalized) or *endommagée* (ah-dom-ma-zhay) (damaged). Theft or damage should be immediately reported to the police. Call the appropriate emergency number (17 or 112), and report: *On m'a volé/vandalisé ma voiture.* (oh ma vo-lay/vah-da-lee-zay ma vwa-tUr) (My car was stolen/vandalized.) You will probably have to follow up with a visit to the *commisariat* to make *une déclaration de vol* (a theft report), and you will, of course, remain in contact with your car rental company and your own insurance company.

Other reasons to call the police are *le vol du sac à main* (leuh vol dU sak a mih) (purse-snatching), *le vol de bijoux* (leuh vol deuh bee-zhoo) (jewelry theft), *le vol du passeport* (leuh vol dU pas-por) (passport theft), and *le vol d'un portefeuille* (leuh vol duh port-feuhy) (wallet theft).

On m'a volé mon sac.	My purse was stolen.
oh ma vo-lay moh sak	
On m'a volé mes bijoux.	My jewelry was stolen.
oh ma vo-lay may bee-zhoo	
On m'a volé mon passeport.	My passport was stolen.
oh ma vo-lay moh pas-por	
On m'a volé mon portefeuille.	My wallet was stolen.
oh ma vo-lay moh port-feuhy	

 C'est urgent. *(say tUr-zhah):* It's urgent.

If you find yourself in a situation where you must make an emergency call, carry the following *numéros d'urgence* with you: 17 for *la police* (la po-lees) (a police emergency), 17 or 112 for *la gendarmerie* (la zhah-dar-mree) (rural and suburban police), 18 for *les pompiers* (lay poh-pyay) (the fire department), and 15 for the *SAMU* (sa-mU) (a medi-cal/paramedic/ambulance emergency). These numbers are all free and direct; they do not require *une télécarte* (Un tay-lay-kart) (a phone card) in a pay phone, just be sure to say: *C'est urgent!* (It's urgent!)

La police, s'il vous plaît.	The police, please.
la po-lees seel voo play	
Les pompiers, s'il vous plaît.	The fire department, please.
le poh-pyay seel voo play	
Le SAMU, s'il vous plaît.	Medical emergency, please.
leuh sa-mU seel voo play	

 Il y a eu un accident. *(eel ya U euh nak-see-dah):* There has been an accident.

Accidents should be reported to the authorities immediately. Use the above sentence if you find yourself in an accident or if you are *témoin* (tay-mwih) (witness) to one. If you see that people are hurt, report *Il y a des blessés.* (eel ya day bles-say) (There are injured people.)

Il y a des blessés.	There are injured people.
eel ya day bles-say	

 Envoyez... s'il vous plaît. *(ah-vwa-yay seel voo play):* Please send . . .

This simple phrase can help you convey urgent messages such as: *Envoyez une ambulance immédiatement!* (ah-vwa-yay Un ah-bU-lahs ee-may-dyat-mah) (Send an ambulance immediately!), *Envoyez la police!* (ah-vwa-yay la po-lees) (Send the police!), or *Envoyez les pompiers!* (ah-vwa-yay lay poh-pyay) (Send the fire department!)

Envoyez une ambulance immédiatement!	Send an ambulance immediately!
ah-vwa-yay Un ah-bU-lahs ee-may-dyat-mah	
Envoyez la police!	Send the police!
ah-vwa-yay la po-lees	
Envoyez les pompiers!	Send the fire department!
ah-vwa-yay lay poh-pyay	

 Il y a eu un cambriolage. *(eel ya U uh kah-bree-o-lazh):* There has been a burglary.

Approximately five hundred home robberies occur daily in France; most of them take place through front doors. Be sure to keep your door locked at all times. If you fall victim to this crime, leave the premises untouched, and call the police to report *Il y a eu un cambriolage.* (eel ya U uh kah-bree-o-lazh) (There has been a burglary.) Be prepared to give your address and telephone number.

 Il y a un incendie. *(eel ya euh nih-sah-dee):* There is a fire.

In case of fire, call *les pompiers* (the fire department) and report: *Il y a un incendie.* (eel ya euh nih-sah-dee) (There is a fire.) In case of dire emergency, call for help to anyone within earshot with: *Au secours!* (o skoor) (Help!) or *À l'aide!* (a led) (Help!)

Au secours!	Help!
o skoor	
À l'aide!	Help!
a led	

Chapter 14

Health Issues

Vous avez une intoxication alimentaire. *(voo za-vay Un ih-tok-see-ka-syoh a-lee-mah-ter):* You have food poisoning.

If it is your misfortune to be diagnosed with food poisoning, this is the phrase you will hear. You can then use it to explain to your friends why you are *indisposé(e)* (ih-dees-po-zay) (indisposed). You may want to ask the doctor what diet to follow: *Quel régime est-ce que je dois suivre?* or you can ask if the doctor can prescribe something: *Pouvez-vous me prescrire quelque chose?*

J'ai une intoxication alimentaire.	I have food poisoning.
zhay Un ih-tok-see-ka-syoh a-lee-mah-ter	
Je suis indisposé(e).	I am not feeling well.
zheuh swee ih-dees-po-zay	
Quel régime est-ce que je dois suivre?	What diet should I follow?
kel ray-zheem es keuh zheuh dwa swee-vr	

Pouvez-vous me prescrire   Can you prescribe me something?
    quelque chose?
poo-vay-voo meuh prays-kreer
    kel-keuh shoz

 J'ai mal... *(zhay mal)*: I ache . . .

Should you have *de petits problèmes de santé* (minor health problems), the phrase *J'ai mal...* will prove very useful, either *à la pharmacie* (at the pharmacy), *chez le dentiste* (at a dentist's), or *chez le médecin* (at a doctor's office). If you have a toothache, tell the dentist: *J'ai mal aux dents.* (I have a toothache.) If you have a headache, say: *J'ai mal à la tête.* If your throat hurts, say: *J'ai mal à la gorge.*

J'ai mal à la tête.   I have a headache.
zhay mal a la tet
J'ai mal à la gorge.   I have a sore throat.
zhay mal a la gorzh
J'ai mal aux dents.   I have a toothache.
zhay mal o dah

 Je me sens... *(zheuh meuh sah)*: I feel . . .

If you feel you are getting sick, but do not know the exact cause, use either of these phrases: *Je me sens mal* (I feel ill) or *Je ne me sens pas très bien.* (I don't feel very well.) When you simply feel nauseated, and you don't know exactly what's wrong, use this phrase: *J'ai mal au cœur.* Note that even though this phrase refers to *le coeur* (the heart), it does not imply that there is anything wrong with your heart.

When you feel better, say: *Je me sens mieux.* (I feel better.)

Je me sens mal.   I feel sick.

zheuh meuh sah mal

Je ne me sens pas très bien.   I do not feel very well.

zheuh neuh meuh sah pa tray byeh

J'ai mal au cœur.   I feel nauseated.

zhay mal o keuhr

Je me sens mieux.   I feel better.

zheuh meuh sah myeuh

 Je ne suis pas dans mon assiette. *(zheuh neuh swee pa dah mo na-syet):* I am not feeling right.

Another way to express that one does not feel well is to use this colorful phrase: *Je ne suis pas dans mon assiette* (literally, I am not in my plate; in other words, I don't feel right).

 J'ai de la fièvre. *(zhay deuh la fye-vr):* I have a fever.

If you have a fever, tell your doctor *J'ai de la fièvre.* This could signal that you have *un rhume* (uh rUm) (a cold), or worse, *la grippe* (la greep) (the flu). Either way you may need to inform your friends that you are sick: *Je suis malade.* (zheuh swee ma-lad) If you have *une toux* (Un too) (a cough), you might need to get *du sirop* (dU see-ro) (cough syrup) or some other *médicament* (may-dee-ka-mah) (medication). You may even need to call *un docteur/un médecin* (uh dok-teuhr/uh mayd-sih) (a doctor).

J'ai un rhume.   I have a cold.

zhay uh rUm

J'ai la grippe.   I have the flu.

zhay la greep

J'ai une toux.   I have a cough.

zhay Un too

Je suis malade.   I am sick.

zheuh swee ma-lad

 Il me faut une pharmacie. *(eel meuh fo Un far-ma-see)*: I
need a pharmacy.

For medication for minor ailments such as headaches, ask for directions to a pharmacy by saying: *Il me faut une pharmacie.* (I need a
pharmacy.) If the closest pharmacy is closed, look for a sign on the
door that indicates which neighborhood pharmacy is *de garde* (on
call). French pharmacists are qualified to treat minor health problems
and are usually very helpful. If you have a headache, say: *Il me faut de
l'aspirine.* (I need aspirin.) If you have a cough, say: *Il me faut du sirop
pour la toux.* If the pharmacist thinks you need a doctor, he/she will
tell you: *Il vous faut un médecin.* (eel voo fo tuh mayd-sih) (You need
a doctor.)

Finally, if you have a toothache, tell someone: *Il me faut un dentiste.*
(I need a dentist.)

Il me faut des aspirines.   I need some aspirin.

eel meuh fo day zas-pee-reen

Il me faut un sirop pour la toux.   I need cough syrup.

eel meuh fo tuh see-ro poor la too

Il me faut un docteur/un médecin. I need a doctor.

eel meuh fo tuh dok-teuhr/tuh

   mayd-sih

116

Il me faut un dentiste.
eel meuh fo tuh dah-teest

I need a dentist.

 Où est la pharmacie la plus proche? *(oo ay la far-ma-see la plU prosh):* Where is the closest pharmacy?

Nothing in France is easier to spot than cafés—and pharmacies. The pharmacy's regulatory lighted (often flashing) sign features a green and blue cross. If the green cross is lit, the pharmacy is open. You will find several green crosses on any French street. The French pharmacy experience is not to be missed. Inside, find the plate-glass window *conseils pharmaciens* (pharmaceutical advice), and do not hesitate to approach the pharmacist. The French pharmacist is expected to spend a lot of time with customers, patiently explaining and reassuring them. This is easy to understand in light of the fact that France has a much admired universal health care system which not only allows but encourages people to visit doctors and take good care of their health. The French can afford the cost of medication because the government controls prices. No wonder the French make frequent visits to the pharmacy to have their *ordonnances* (prescriptions) filled.

The other services provided by a *pharmacie* are comparable to those at a typical American pharmacy or drugstore; they include selling over-the-counter medications, hair care products, and other toiletries. The big difference is the level of service you will get in a French pharmacy. Most French pharmacies will prepare products such as specially formulated *shampooings* (shampoos) for your type of hair (look for the word *préparation* on the window). Another big difference is that you will not find any food sold at a pharmacy.

117

Voilà mon ordonnance.   Here is my prescription.

vwa-la mo nor-do-nahs

Un petit conseil, s'il vous plaît.   A little advice, please.

uh peuh-tee koh-say seel voo play

 Essayez l'herboristerie. *(es-say-yay ler-bo-rees-tree):* Try the herbal product pharmacy.

Les médicaments homéopathiques (homeopathic remedies) are commonly used by the French. Pharmacists and physicians recommend them and the national health system reimburses the cost of some of them. Therefore, plant-based health and medicinal products, as well as plant-based beauty products, abound in French pharmacies. These pharmacies will identify themselves as *pharmacies homéopathiques* or *herboristeries.* Some of these stores specialize in a specific area like *les parfums* (perfumes). Do not be surprised to see name permutations such as: *pharmacie-droguerie-herboristerie, pharmacie-droguerie-parfumerie,* or *pharmacie-homéopathique-aromathérapique.* This reflects the great variety of products sold and made in pharmacies and the variety of services offered in addition to filling doctors' prescriptions.

la pharmacie homéopathique   homeopathic pharmacy

la far-ma-see o-may-o-pa-teek

la pharmacie-droguerie-   pharmacy-drugstore-perfume store
　　parfumerie

la far-ma-see dro-gree par-fU-mree

la pharmacie aromathérapique   aromatherapy pharmacy

la far-ma-see a-ro-ma-tay-ra-peek

Y a-t-il un hôpital? *(ya teel uhn no-pee-tal):* Is there a hospital?

For a serious (enough) medical issue that is not an extreme emergency, ask this question: *Il y a un hôpital pas trop loin d'ici?* (Is there a hospital not too far from here?) When you arrive at the hospital, follow the sign *Accueil* (Admissions).

The French have a universal health care system, but care is no longer totally paid for by the state. French citizens carry a *Carte Vitale*, which entitles them to a 70 percent reimbursement of all medical bills. The remaining amount is either paid out of pocket or by a supplemental policy which most people have through a professional association or private insurance company. As a tourist, you will hopefully have your own *assurance médicale* (medical insurance) from your home country and/or through your travel plan.

As an alternative to calling *le SAMU* (the ambulance service), you should know that in France *les pompiers* (firemen) perform accident services, providing rapid response for medical emergencies, injuries, and road accidents, as well as fires.

Y a-t-il un hôpital pas trop loin d'ici? ya teel euh no-pee-tal pa tro lwih dee-see	Is there a hospital not too far from here?
Où est l'accueil? oo ay la-keuhy	Where is Admissions?

Chapter 15

Making Plans

 Prenons rendez-vous. *(preuh-noh rah-day-voo)*: Let's make a date.

Have you made friends In Paris or in another French-speaking town? *Magnifique!* (Wonderful!) You will now have to set up times and places, when and where your *rendez-vous* (dates/meetings) will take place. You may want to meet them at a *café* or *bar*. That is, after all, where *tout Paris* (all of Paris) lives outside of work and school. Or you may want to meet in front of the *musée* (museum) or any other tourist site you're visiting that day. Perhaps you would prefer to be picked up *à l'hôtel* (at the hotel) where you're staying and will wait for your acquaintance in the lobby. Don't forget to set *l'heure du rendez-vous* (the time of your meeting)!

Prenons rendez-vous pour quatre heures.   Let's make a date for four o'clock.

preuh-noh rah-day-voo poor
    kat-reuhr

Prenons rendez-vous chez Paul!   Let's meet at Paul's place!
preuh-noh rah-day-voo shay pol

 Viens me chercher! *(vyeh meuh sher-shay)*: Come pick me up!

If your friend offers to pick you up before going out to dinner or the movies: *Tu veux que je te cherche?* (tU veuh keuh zheuh teuh shersh), say: *Oui, viens me chercher à l'hôtel* (wee vyeh meuh sher-shay a lo-tel) (Yes, come get me at the hotel), or *Oui, viens me chercher au bureau.* (wee vyeh meuh sher-shay o bU-ro) (Yes, come get me at the office.)

If you would like your friend to pick you up at the train station or at the airport, say: *Viens me chercher à la gare/à l'aéroport, s'il te plaît.* (vyeh meuh sher-shay a la gar/a lay-ro-por seel teuh play)

Viens me chercher à l'hôtel!   Come pick me up at the hotel!
vyeh meuh sher-shay a lo-tel

Viens me chercher au bureau!   Come get me at the office!
vyeh meuh sher-shay o bU-ro

Cherche-moi à la gare!   Pick me up at the train station!
shersh mwa a la gar

Cherche-moi à l'aéroport!   Pick me up at the airport!
shersh mwa a la-ay-ro-por

 Je serai au bar. *(zheuh seuh-ray o bar):* I will be at the bar.

When your date is going to pick you up, you may want to be precise about where and when you will be ready. For example, if you plan to be ready at 7 P.M., say: *Je serai prêt/prête à dix-neuf heures.* If you plan to wait at the bar, say: *Je serai au bar.* If you want to assure your friend that you will be on time, say: *Je serai à l'heure.*

Je serai prêt/prête à dix-neuf   I will be ready at 7 P.M.
   heures.
zheuh seuh-ray pray/pret a deez-
   neuh veuhr

Je serai à l'heure.   I will be on time.
zheuh seuh-ray a leuhr

 Attends-moi! *(a-tah mwa):* Wait for me!

If you are running late for your date, call your friend, and say: *Je suis en retard mais j'arrive. Attends-moi, s'il te plait!* (zheuh swee ah reuh-tar may zha-reev a-tah mwa seel teuh play) (I'm late, but I'm on the way. Please wait for me!)

   If you plan to meet your friend at the movies, and you know that he/she will get there before you, say: *Attends-moi devant le ciné!* (Wait for me in front of the theater!)

   Let's suppose you know you'll arrive first, say, for example: *Je t'attendrai dans le lobby de l'hôtel.* (I will wait for you in the hotel lobby.) If you think your friend may not be very punctual, say: *Ne me fais pas trop attendre!* (Don't make me wait too long!)

Attends-moi devant le ciné!   Wait for me in front of the theater!
a-tah mwa deuh-vah leuh see-nay

Je t'attendrai dans le lobby   I will wait for you in the hotel lobby.
   de l'hôtel.
zheuh tat-tah-dray dah leuh
   lob-bee deuh lo-tel

Ne me fais pas trop attendre!   Don't make me wait too long!
neuh meuh fay pa tro a-tah-dr

Rejoins-moi! *(reuh-zhwih mwa):* Meet me!

If you're really excited about something you are doing or about where you are, call your friend, and say: *Rejoins-moi vite!* (reuh-zhwih mwa veet) (Meet me right away!) If you are at Paulette's place, and you would like your friend to meet you there, say *Rejoins-moi chez Paulette*. If you are enjoying the lively atmosphere of the *place du Tertre* in Montmartre, and you want your friend to meet you there, say: *Rejoins-moi à la place du Tertre!* (Meet me at the *place du Tertre*!)

Rejoins-moi chez Paulette!	Meet me at Paulette's!
reuh-zhwih mwa shay po-let	
Rejoins-moi à la place du Tertre!	Meet me at the *place du Tertre*!
reuh-zhwih mwa a la plas dU ter-tr	

 J'espère te revoir. *(zhes-per teuh reuh-vwar):* I hope to see you again.

This is a phrase that can be used in many contexts. You can end a letter or a phone conversation with *J'espère te revoir bientôt.* (zhes-per teuh reuh-vwar byeh-to) (I hope to see you again soon.) If your friends ask whether you will come back to visit soon, tell them: *J'espère bien.* (I sure hope so.) The adverb *bien* tends to soften the meaning of a verb. For example: *Je t'aime* (zheuh tem) (I love you) versus *Je t'aime bien* (zheuh tem byeh) (I like you). However, in the case of *espérer*, it has the opposite effect: *J'espère bien* is a much more assertive manner of expressing that you *do* hope so.

If you expect a positive answer to a request or perhaps to a job application, show moderate anticipation and hope by stating *J'ai bon espoir* which conveys the idea that you are hopeful without being overly optimistic.

J'espère bien.	I sure hope so.
zhes-per byeh	
J'ai bon espoir.	I am hopeful.
zhay bon es-pwar	
Je compte sur toi.	I am counting on you.
zheuh koht sUr twa	
Je t'attendrai.	I will expect you.
zheuh tat-tah-dray	

 On pourrait... *(oh poo-ray):* We could . . .

Shopping, dining, visiting, attending a concert or a show are all integral parts of spending a great time in France. There are an enormous number of choices, and quality is often world class. When planning to go out with friends, feel free to make suggestions as to what you would like to do. You will find many uses for the handy little phrase *On pourrait...* which clearly suggests what one might do without being too pushy or bossy.

On pourrait faire du shopping.	We could go shopping.
oh poo-ray fer dU shop-peeng	
On pourrait aller dîner.	We could go out for dinner.
oh poo-ray ta-lay dee-nay	
On pourrait aller à une exposition.	We could go to an exhibit.
oh poo-ray ta-lay a un eks-po-zee-syoh	

On pourrait aller au cinéma.	We could go to the movies.
oh poo-ray ta-lay o see-nay-ma	
On pourrait faire les clubs.	We could go clubbing.
oh poo-ray fer lay kleuhb	
On pourrait se promener.	We could go for a walk.
oh poo-ray seuh prom-nay	

 R.S.V.P. *(er-es-vay-pay)*: R.S.V.P.

R.S.V.P. is an abbreviation for the French phrase, *Répondez, s'il vous plaît,* which translates as "Please reply." If you receive a written invitation, especially from a French person, be sure to reply in writing. You may use the enclosed *carton-réponse* (reply card) if you received one, or provide your own card, but in any event you must reply. When you reply, use one of the following phrases: *J'accepte avec plaisir* (I gladly accept) or *Je regrette de ne pouvoir être des vôtres.* (I regret I cannot join you.)

Coming a few minutes late when you're invited to someone's home (fifteen minutes is the norm) is normal and even expected. Showing up early is considered a *faux pas*.

Whenever you are formally invited to someone's home, it is customary, just as in the United States, to bring a house gift: *des fleurs* (flowers), *des bonbons* (candy), or *une bouteille de vin* (a bottle of wine) to your hosts. Upon arriving, give your gift to the hostess or to the host and say: *Permettez-moi de vous offrir ce petit cadeau.* (Allow me to give you this little gift.)

J'accepte avec plaisir.	I gladly accept.
zhak-sept a-vek play-zeer	

Je regrette de ne pouvoir être
des vôtres.
zheuh reuh-gret deuh neuh
    poo-vwar etr day votr

I regret I cannot join you.

Permettez-moi de vous offrir
ce petit cadeau.
per-met-tay mwa deuh voo zo-freer
    seuh peuh-tee ka-do

Allow me to give you this little gift.

 Ça vous dérangerait si on se tutoyait? *(sa voo day-rah-zhray see oh seuh tU-twa-yay):* Would you mind if we start using the familiar *tu*?

Shaking hands is a must in French company when you say hello and good-bye. A brief encounter is often punctuated by two handshakes, one to start and one to finish. If you get really engaged in a conversation with a person you do not know well, try to avoid topics such as religion, marital status, or income, which are considered to be of a very personal nature. However, for the French *la politique* (politics) is a favorite topic for discussion and may be hard to avoid!

When you meet a person for the first time, and while you're getting acquainted, be sure to use the *vous* form of address, for example, when you thank him/her for an invitation or when you pay compliments. After a while, you might be asked, or you yourself might be ready to ask, the following question: *Ça vous dérangerait si on se tutoyait?* (Would you mind if we addressed each other using the familiar *tu*?) Note that a nonnative speaker usually waits to be asked. This suggestion indicates that your new friend is ready to enter more familiar ground. However, the use of *tu* does not mean that you may begin asking very personal questions, such as what a person earns.

When meeting again, even for the second time, don't be surprised if you are kissed on the cheek or cheeks by French acquaintances, both men and women. You will soon learn to *donner la bise* yourself.

Je vous remercie de votre invitation.
zheuh voo reuh-mer-see deuh vot rih-vee-ta-syoh

I thank you for your invitation.

Vous avez une très belle maison.
voo za-vay Un tray bel may-zoh

You have a very beautiful house.

Ça ne me dérangerait pas du tout.
sa neuh meuh day-rah-zhray pa dU too

It would not bother me at all.

Chapter 16

Romance

 Tu es vraiment sympa. *(tU ay vray-mah sih-pa)*: You are really nice.

If you're lucky enough to meet a very special person toward whom you feel attracted and whom you wish to get to know better, you will want to express your nascent interest by paying a few compliments to your new "heartthrob." You can say that you find him/her *sympa* (nice), *mignon/mignonne* (cute), or even *adorable* (adorable) or *beau /belle/attirant/attirante* (handsome/beautiful/attractive). A slightly more daring approach would be to say that you like the person a lot. In that case, note that a French native speaker would most likely use the idiomatic phrase *Tu me plais* (literally translated as: You please me). The word-for-word translation of "I love you" is *Je t'aime* (zheuh tem), but that utterance has a deep and intense meaning likely to shock someone you only recently met.

Tu es mignon/mignonne. tU ay mee-nyoh/mee-nyon	You are cute.
Tu es adorable. tU ay za-do-ra-bl	You are adorable.

Tu es attirant/attirante.   You are attractive.

tu ay za-tee-rah/za-tee-raht

Tu me plais beaucoup.   I like you a lot.

tU meuh play bo-koo

 Voudrais-tu sortir avec moi? *(voo-dray tU sor-teer a-vek mwa)*: Would you like to go out with me?

Assuming the special person you met appears to reciprocate your interest, it may be time to ask him/her to go out with you for coffee, a drink, or dinner. Note that the phrase *prendre un pot* does not necessarily imply having an alcoholic drink, it can refer to any drink, including coffee or soda. If you want to use a direct approach to ask the person out, use the phrase *Voudrais-tu sortir avec moi?* If you want to use a softer, less direct approach, say: *Ça te dirait de sortir avec moi?* The use of the conditional form of the verb *dire* in these phrases conveys that you are not taking his/her answer for granted. Using *Ça te dirait* is more like saying: Does it seem like a good idea to you?

Voudrais-tu dîner avec moi?   Would you like to have dinner

voo-dray tU dee-nay a-vek mwa   with me?

Ça te dirait de sortir avec moi?   Would you feel like going out

sa teuh dee-ray deuh sor-teer   with me?

    a-vek mwa

As-tu envie de prendre un pot?   Would you like to have a drink?

a tU ah-vee deuh prah-dr uh po

Je t'invite à déjeuner.   I'm inviting you to lunch.

zheuh tih-veet a day-zheuh-nay

Peut-on se revoir? *(peuh-toh seuh reuh-vwar)*: Can we see each other again?

Now that the introductions have been completed, you've spent time together, and your mutual feelings are clear, the next step would be to ask to see your friend again. Use this low-key phrase *Peut-on se revoir?* (Can we see each other again?), or be more forthright and ask *Quand/Où est-ce qu'on peut se revoir?* (When/Where can we see each other again?) You might even express how impatient you are for another meeting by using the phrase: *J'ai hâte de te revoir* (I am anxious/impatient to see you again) or by expressing how much you will miss your new friend: *Tu vas me manquer.* (tU va meuh mah-kay) (I'll miss you.) Be very careful to use this phrase correctly, or you will declare that it is your friend who's going to miss you, instead of your missing him/her. The phrase *Tu vas me manquer*, literally translated, means: You will be missed (by me).

Quand/Où peut-on se revoir?	When/Where can we see each
kah/oo peuh-toh seuh reuh-vwar	other again?
J'ai hâte de te revoir.	I can't wait to see you again.
zhay at deuh teuh reuh-vwar	
Tu vas me manquer.	I am going to miss you.
tU va meuh mah-kay	

 J'ai le cœur qui bat la chamade. *(zhay leuh keuhr kee ba la sha-mad)*: My heart is beating like a drum.

You could use this phrase when you are extremely emotional and your heart is indeed beating like a drum. This could apply to a person receiving a proposal of marriage, as well as to the one doing the asking: *Son cœur battait la chamade.* (His/Her heart was beating like a drum.)

As in English, there are many romantic expressions in French that use the heart as a metaphor for emotions. A person whose heart has been broken will say: *J'ai le cœur brisé* (I have a broken heart) or *Mon cœur a été brisé en mille morceaux.* (My heart was broken into a thousand pieces.)

Another common phrase which also invokes the heart, used in happy or "warm" moments, is: *Ça me fait chaud au cœur.* (It warms my heart./It makes me feel good.)

J'ai le cœur brisé.	I have a broken heart.
zhay leuh keuhr bree-zay	
Mon cœur a été brisé en	My heart has been broken into a
mille morceaux.	thousand pieces.
moh keuhr a ay-tay bree-zay ah	
meel mor-so	
Ça me fait chaud au cœur.	It warms my heart.
sa meuh fay sho o keuhr	

 Tu es mon chéri. *(tU ay moh shay-ree):* You are my darling.

This tender phrase is used toward both men and women, although a man may also use the feminine equivalent *Tu es ma chérie* (tU ay ma shay-ree) to say: You are my darling. Taking this term of endearment to a higher level would yield this phrase: *Tu es mon amour* (You are my love) which, once again, may be addressed to a man or a woman. As in English, you may call a loved one *mon petit cœur* (my dear heart).

There are numerous terms of endearment in all languages; these may be of a very personal nature. Some common French phrases you may hear will refer to a specific animal, such as: *mon petit canard* (moh peuh-tee ka-nar) (my little duckling); *mon poussin* (moh poo-sih) (my chick); *mon petit lapin* (moh peuh-tee la-pih) (my little bunny); and even *ma petite souris* (ma peuh-teet soo-ree) (my little mouse). To make them sound even sweeter, these terms are often modified, as in: *mon canard en sucre* (moh ka-nar ah sU-kr) (my sugar duckling) or *mon lapin en chocolat* (moh la-pih ah sho-ko-la) (my chocolate bunny). Uniquely French is the phrase *mon chou* (moh shoo), a phrase which, again, you may use toward both men and women. Literally translated, this term means "my cabbage," but it more likely refers back to *un chou à la crème* (uh shoo a la krem) (a cream puff). As usual, a French word sounds much cuter when it doubles a syllable (i.e., a *bonbon* is a "goody-goody"); therefore, *mon chouchou* (moh shoo-shoo) is twice as cute as *mon chou*. Another derivative of this phrase is *mon petit bout de chou* (moh peuh-tee boo deuh shoo) (my little bit of cream puff). The assumption here is that the smaller something is, the cuter it is.

Tu es mon amour.	You are my love.
tU ay mo na-moor	
Tu es mon petit cœur.	You are my dear heart.
tU ay moh peuh-tee keuhr	
Tu es mon chou.	You are my cream puff.
tU ay moh shoo	
Tu es mon petit bout de chou.	You are my little cream puff.
tU ay moh peuh-tee boo deuh shoo	

Je t'aime. *(zheuh tem)* I love you.

There are many variations of the quintessential phrase *Je t'aime* (I love you). If you want to make it clear that you like a person, and that it is not romantic love you are expressing, simply say: *Je t'aime bien*. If, on the other hand, you are indeed passionately in love, say: *Je t'aime passionnément*. Since strong emotions are said to drive people *à la folie* (to madness) or *à mourir* (to death), there are several typical French expressions which address this notion.

Je t'aime bien.	I like you.
zheuh tem byeh	
Je t'aime passionnément.	I love you passionately.
zheuh tem pa-syon-nay-mah	
Je t'aime infiniment.	My love for you is infinite.
zheuh tem ih-fee-nee-mah	
Je t'aime à la folie.	I love you madly.
zheuh tem a la fo-lee	
Je suis amoureux fou/amoureuse	I am madly in love with you.
folle de toi.	
zheuh swee a-moo-reuh foo/	
a-moo-reuhz fol deuh twa	
Je t'aime à mourir.	I love you to death.
zheuh tem a moo-reer	

 Je t'embrasse. *(zheuh tah-bras):* Love. (To close a letter, etc.)

The phrase *Je t'embrasse* is often used at the end of a phone conversation or any written communication and has the same meaning as "Love you/Love ya" for an American, even though its literal meaning is: "I kiss you." Sometimes the phrase is modified for emphasis to: *Je t'embrasse fort* (as in, "I'm giving you a big hug").

In greeting good friends, the French give one another *des bises* (little kisses) on the cheeks, while Americans give each other *des étreintes* (hugs). How many *bises* on the cheeks you will receive from your French friends depends on what region they are from: the norm is two, one on each cheek, but it can be three or four. The word *bises* or its derivatives *bisous* (tiny kisses) and *grosses bises* (big fat kisses) can be used in conversation as well as at the end of a letter or e-mail message. The verbs *donner un baiser* (to give a kiss) as well as *embrasser* (to kiss) are generic phrases which could mean to give a friendly, motherly, or even a romantic kiss.

Bons baisers (literally, good kisses) is often written at the end of a letter; again, this has the same meaning as "Love" for Americans. It is used between close friends and relations. With more casual acquaintances, the closing phrases *Amicalement* and *Mes amitiés* are more suitable, as they express simple friendship. We can observe cultural differences in the ways the French and the Americans express "Love." The French language seems to focus on the external expression of love, while American English focuses on the feelings conveyed. That's why it's difficult to give culturally appropriate translations for most of these phrases.

Bons baisers.	Love.
boh bay-zay	
Amicalement.	Best regards.
a-mee-kal-mah	
Mes amitiés.	Best regards.
may za-mee-tyay	

Chapter 17

Keeping in Touch

 Quelles sont les heures d'ouverture du bureau de poste?
(kel soh lay zeuhr doo-ver-tUr dU bU-ro deuh post): What are the post office hours?

La Poste (the French post office) is generally *ouverte de neuf heures à dix-sept heures* (open from 9 A.M. to 5 P.M.) during the work week and also Saturday mornings. In villages and small towns, the post office may be closed during lunchtime. *Les heures d'ouverture* (business hours) are always posted outside the post office.

In Paris, *le bureau de poste central est ouvert vingt-quatre heures sur vingt-quatre* (the main post office is open twenty-four hours a day).

Ouvert du lundi au samedi.	Open from Monday through
oo-ver dU luh-dee o sam-dee	Saturday.
Le bureau de poste est fermé	The post office is closed on Sundays.
le dimanche.	
leuh bU-ro deuh post ay fer-may	
le dee-mahsh	

Les heures d'ouverture sont affichées.	Business hours are posted.
lay zeuhr doo-ver-tUr soh ta-fee-shay	
Le bureau central est ouvert vingt-quatre heures sur vingt-quatre.	The main office is open twenty-four hours a day.
leuh bU-ro sah-tral ay too-ver vih-kat reuhr sUr vih-katr	

 C'est combien, l'affranchissement pour les États-Unis?

(say koh-byeh la-frah-shees-mah poor lay zay-ta-zU-nee): How much is the postage for the United States?

Because postage stamps are easily available at *tabacs* (tobacco shops) and even supermarkets, tourists and visitors will use the post office mostly to send parcels. French post offices are easy to spot; they have bright yellow mailboxes and signs out front. Inside each post office you are likely to find *les guichets automatiques* (automated sales machines) with instructions also in English. You can use them to weigh *les paquets/les colis* (packages) and buy stamps; stamp machines are marked *affranchissement*. If you feel more comfortable talking to a clerk, *il faut faire la queue* (you must get in line). Ask the clerk: *C'est combien pour un timbre?* (How much is it for a stamp?) or *C'est combien, l'affranchissement pour les États-Unis?* (How much is the postage for the United States?)

If you want to send a package airmail, tell the clerk: *Je veux envoyer ce paquet/ce colis aux États-Unis par avion.* (I want to send this package/parcel to the United States via airmail.)

C'est combien pour un timbre?	How much is it for a stamp?
say koh-byeh por uh tih-br	
C'est combien, l'affranchissement pour les États-Unis?	How much is the postage for the United States?
say koh-byeh la-frah-shees-mah poor lay zay-ta-zU-nee	
Je veux envoyer ce paquet aux États-Unis par avion.	I want to send this package to the United States via airmail.
zheuh veuh ah-vwa-yay seuh pa-kay o zay-ta-zU-nee par a-vyoh	

 Je voudrais faire des copies. (*zheuh voo-dray fer day ko-pee*): I would like to make copies.

Remember that, in France, people also use their *PTT* (*Poste Télégraphe Téléphone*) (post office) for a variety of services, such as using *Minitel* and Internet stations (*Cyberposte*). The *Minitel* is a French information network; unlike the Internet, it is only accessible in France. Nowadays, its use is increasingly limited to online sales and to administrative procedures, especially in education. *Cyberposte* is an Internet-enabled kiosk available in post offices. It allows easy Internet access to anyone with *une carte d'accès* (a smart/memory card). The French *PTT* installed this service in over a thousand post offices around the country to provide Internet access to those who do not have it at home or at work. Other services offered by *La Poste* include funds transfers, bill paying, check cashing, photocopies, faxes, and phone calls. With their myriad services, post offices attract almost every French citizen. Therefore, as a tourist, it's wise to avoid the post office at lunchtime and in the late afternoon when many local workers take care of personal business at their closest *PTT*.

If your hotel does not offer services such as sending faxes, or if you wish to avoid the high hotel fees, find a *bureau de poste*, wait in line, and say: *Je voudrais envoyer une télécopie.* (I would like to send a fax.) For other services, say: *Je voudrais toucher un chèque* (I would like to cash a check) or *Je voudrais faire un appel international.* (I would like to make an international phone call.) Be aware that the lines may be long; but once you reach *le guichet* (window), don't hesitate to ask whatever questions you have.

Je voudrais envoyer une télécopie.
I would like to send a fax.

zheuh voo-dray ah-vwa-yay Un tay-lay-ko-pee

Je voudrais toucher un chèque.
I would like to cash a check.

zheuh voo-dray too-shay uh shek

Je voudrais faire un appel international.
I would like to make an international phone call.

zheuh voo-dray fer euh na-pel ih-ter-na-syo-nal

 Vous désirez le service *Poste restante*? *(voo day-see-ray leuh ser-vees post res-taht):* Would you like the *Poste Restante* service?

The phrase *Poste restante* refers to a service offered by *La Poste* where it holds mail until the recipient comes in to pick it up. This service is often used by people on the go who have no way of having mail delivered directly to their place of residence at a given time. Mail sent to a *Poste restante* address should include the name of the person, followed by the phrase *Poste restante* and must also include the name and *le code postal de la ville ou du quartier* (zip code of the city or neighborhood). To pick up your mail from *Poste restante*, you'll need to show a passport or other ID. There may be a small charge for the service.

Oui merci, c'est une bonne idée.   Yes, thanks, that's a good idea.
wee mer-see say tUn bon ee-day

 Passez-moi un coup de fil! *(pa-say mwa uh koo deuh feel)*: Call me!

This essential phrase means the same thing as *Téléphonez-moi* or *Appelez-moi* but is less formal. You may even hear it from a new acquaintance. If he/she uses this expression, you'll know that you are considered a friend.

Téléphonez-moi!   Call me!
tay-lay-fo-nay mwa
Appelez-moi!   Call me!
ap-lay mwa

 Allô, bonjour. C'est John à l'appareil. *(a-lo boh-zhoor say zhah a la-pa-ray)*: Hello, good morning, this is John.

When you phone someone, first say the customary: *Allô, bonjour* (Hello); then state your name, for example: *C'est John à l'appareil.* (This is John calling.) If you don't recognize the voice, ask: *Qui est à l'appareil, s'il vous plaît?* (Who's on the line, please?/Who's calling, please?)

Qui est à l'appareil?	Who's calling?
kee ay ta la-pa-ray	
Qui est à l'appareil, s'il vous plaît?	Who is on the line, please?
kee ay ta la-pa-ray seel voo play	

 Vous avez le mauvais numéro. *(voo za-vay leuh mo-vay nU-may-ro):* You have the wrong number.

If you hear *Vous avez le mauvais numéro*, you dialed the wrong number. In other circumstances, you may be told: *Attendez, s'il vous plaît*; *Un moment, s'il vous plaît*; or *Ne quittez pas, s'il vous plaît* (Please wait/hold). If you called a business, you are more likely to hear the more formal phrase: *Veuillez patienter, s'il vous plaît.* (Stay on the line, please.)

If you place a call and get no response, you may wish to call *l'opératrice* (the operator).

Veuillez patienter.	Please hold.
veuh-yay pa-syah-tay	
Attendez, s'il vous plaît.	One moment, please./Please wait.
at-tah-day seel voo play	
Un moment, s'il vous plaît.	One moment, please.
uh mo-mah seel voo play	
Ne quittez pas, s'il vous plaît.	Stay on the line, please.
neuh kee-tay pa seel voo play	

Cet abonné est sur la liste rouge. *(set a-bo-nay ay sUr la leest roozh):* This subscriber is unlisted.

France Télécom subscribers have several choices concerning the listing of their phone number and related information. A subscriber may request to be on their *liste orange*: This guarantees that their information will not be divulged to marketing groups. Or subscribers may request to be on the *liste chamoix*: This means that their information is unlisted and unpublished but may be obtained through information services. A third choice is to be on the *liste rouge*, which gives total privacy and prevents access to information by any and all parties.

Cet abonné est sur la liste orange.	This subscriber's information
set a-bo-nay ay sUr la leest o-rahzh	is restricted.
Cet abonné est sur la liste chamoix.	This subscriber's number is not published.
set a-bo-nay ay sUr la leest sha-mwa	

Je veux faire un appel en PCV. *(zheuh veuh fer euh na-pel ah pay-say-vay):* I want to make a collect call.

Use this phrase to make a collect call in France. To make an international collect call, simply dial 00 followed by 33, then enter the country code (1 for the United States or Canada), and finally the rest of the number you wish to dial.

You can make *appels domestiques et internationaux* (domestic and international phone calls) from any *cabine téléphonique* (telephone booth) or *bureau de poste* (post office). You may receive calls on pay phones that display a blue logo of a ringing bell. Pay phones can be found on the street and in other public places throughout France. For calls within France, local or long-distance, simply dial all ten digits of the French *numéro de téléphone*. Note that numbers beginning with 08 00 are toll-free, those beginning with 08 36 are "premium-rate," and those beginning with 06 are mobile phones (and therefore also relatively expensive to call).

Be aware that France is divided into five zones with the following *préfixes régionaux* (area codes): 01 for Paris, 02 for northwest France, 03 for northeast France, 04 for southeast France and the island of Corsica, and 05 for southwest France. These area codes form part of the phone number.

un appel domestique   a domestic call
euh na-pel do-mes-teek
un appel international   an international call
euh na-pel ih-ter-na-syo-nal
le numéro de téléphone   telephone number
leuh nU-may-ro deuh tay-lay-fon
le préfixe régional   area code
leuh pray-fiks ray-zhyo-nal
le préfixe international   country code
leuh pray-fiks ih-ter-na-syo-nal

 Une télécarte à cinquante unités. *(Un tay-lay-kart a sih-kaht U-nee-tay):* A fifty-unit phone card.

Even though everyone in France (including many visitors and tourists) seems to be constantly talking on his/her cell phone, the *télécarte*, a 50- or 120-unit phone card, is readily available. You will need it in order to use pay phones, since coin-operated phones have been phased out. *Télécartes* are available at *tabacs* (tobacco shops), *supermarchés*

(supermarkets), and *kiosques* (newsstands) as well as at *bureaux de poste* (post offices), *syndicats d'initiative* (tourist offices), and also at many *stations de métro et gares* (subway and train stations). Look for a sign that says *Télécarte en vente ici*. (Phone card sold here.)

A *télécarte* has a specific number of units, called *unités*, which are used up as you make calls. Whenever you use your *télécarte*, the remaining amount of credit is displayed, and the decreasing balance can be seen during your call. When it is depleted, just throw the card away, that is, unless you're building a collection. This has indeed become a popular pastime for many, because *France Télécom* prints an endless variety of limited-edition cards featuring beautiful and colorful graphics. Recently, *France Télécom* has started to offer personalized *télécartes* to its customers who can choose images from a large online library or by uploading a photo from their own computers.

Télécarte en vente ici.   Phone card sold here.
tay-lay-kart ah vaht ee-see

 Pouvez-vous me connecter? *(poo-vay voo meuh kon-nek-tay)*: Can you connect me?

Instructions in French telephone booths are also provided in English, but the print is very small, and the steps outlined are not perfectly clear. If you must make your call through a French-speaking operator, use the phrase *Pouvez-vous me connecter?* However, the procedure is usually the following: *décrochez* (pick up the receiver), *insérez votre carte* (insert your card), *attendez la tonalité* (wait for the dial tone), and *composez votre numéro* (dial the number).

Décrochez!	Pick up the receiver!
day-kro-shay	
Insérez votre carte!	Insert your card!
ih-say-ray vo-tr kart	
Attendez la tonalité!	Wait for the dial tone!
a-tah-day la to-na-lee-tay	
Composez votre numéro!	Dial the number!
koh-po-zay votr nU-may-ro	

Je voudrais louer un portable. *(zheuh voo-dray loo-ay uh por-ta-bl):* I would like to rent a cell phone.

Cell phones are available for rental at airports and phone stores. Phones all carry a memory card called a SIM (Subscriber Identity Module). You will generally need to have a new SIM card installed when you enter a different European country. Note that you can save and reinstall an old SIM card, if the calling time is not yet used up.

Les tarifs (rental rates) in France are approximately $25–$50 per week plus charges for placing and receiving each call. The least expensive alternative uses the same service that the French use. You will be paying local rates which are inexpensive and include unlimited, free incoming calls from anywhere in the world. Calls to the United States are about $0.80 per minute. If you decide to rent a phone, ask: *C'est combien le tarif de location*? (How much is the rental?), and explain how long you will need it. If the cell phone you rented for your visit does not work properly, return it, and ask *Puis-je en avoir un qui fonctionne comme il faut?* (May I have another one that works properly?)

C'est combien le tarif de location?   What is the rental fee?
say koh-byeh leuh ta-reef deuh
   lo-ka-syoh

Il me le faut pour un mois.   I need it for a month.
eel meuh leuh fo poor uh mwa

Ce portable ne fonctionne pas   This cell phone does not work
   comme il faut.   properly.
seuh por-ta-bl neuh fohk-syon pa
   kom eel fo

Puis-je en avoir un qui fonctionne   May I have one that works properly?
   comme il faut?
pweezh a na-vwar uh kee fohk-syon
   kom eel fo

Je préfère acheter un portable. *(zheuh pray-fer ash-tay uh por-ta-bl)*: I prefer buying a cell phone.

If keeping in touch with business associates, friends, or relatives is not reason enough to have your own *téléphone portable/téléphone cellulaire* (cell phone) (tay-lay-fon por-ta-bl/tay-lay-fon sel-lU-ler), add to that the fact that many vacation rentals are not equipped with a phone, and that hotels charge high fees for using their land phones. European cell phones work on the GSM standard.

   Upon arriving at the airport, or at any phone store in town, you can purchase a European cell phone with "pre-pay" calling minutes included. After purchase, you will, of course, be able to use your phone on future trips. In addition, many U.S.-based phone plans now offer international service or "unlocking" of your U.S.-made phone. Check into this before departure. You may find, however, that using your U.S.-made GSM phone in Europe is too expensive. Thus, having your own European phone may be the best alternative. Purchased on site, a European GSM cell phone costs as little as forty or fifty euros (a much better deal than ordering it online); units (minutes) may be added at any time, at a phone store or at a *tabac*. As with rental phones, your SIM card will need to be changed when you go to another European country.

Est-ce que je paie pour les appels que je reçois?	Do I pay for incoming calls?
es-keuh zheuh pay poor lay za-pel keuh zheuh reuh-swa	
Quel est le tarif pour des appels aux États-Unis?	What is the rate for calls to the United States?
kel ay leuh ta-reef poor day za-pel o zay-ta-zU-nee	
Quelle garantie est inclue?	What warranty is included?
kel ga-rah-tee ay tih-klU	

 Quelle est la durée de vie de la pile? *(kel ay la dU-ray deuh vee deuh la peel):* What is the life of the battery?

If you do decide to buy a cell phone in France, be sure to ask basic questions such as how long you can expect the battery to last, and whether the phone comes with a replacement battery and a charger. The French use the term *pile* for a disposable battery and the term *batterie* for a rechargeable battery.

Le cellulaire vient avec une batterie de remplacement. leuh sel-lU-ler vyeh a-vek Un ba-tree deuh rah-plas-mah	The cell phone comes with a replacement battery.
Est-ce que vous avez des piles? es-keuh voo za-vay day peel	Do you have batteries?
Où est le rechargeur? oo ay leuh reuh-shar-zheuhr	Where is the charger?

✈ **Il y a des frais d'accès au réseau?** *(eel ya day fray dak-say o ray-zo)*: Is there an access fee to the network?

Remember that along with your new cell phone you must receive and install a SIM card. Also, do not hesitate to ask about voice mail, activation, and cancellation fees. This will save you a lot of confusion when you start using your phone far from the store. Your French SIM card and cell phone service is likely prepaid, so there will be no need for a contract. Your French SIM card will provide you with a French cell phone number. Make sure the store clerk points out your phone number in the documentation or writes it down for you. Note that when you change your SIM card in another country, you will receive a new phone number.

Est-ce qu'il y a des frais d'activation? es-keel ya day fray dak-tee-va-syoh	Is there an activation fee?
Est-ce qu'il y a des frais d'annulation? es-keel ya day fray da-nU-la-syoh	Is there a cancellation fee?

149

**Est-ce que le service permet
l'accès à la messagerie vocale?**
es-keuh leuh ser-vees per-may
lak-say a la may-sa-zhree vo-kal

Does the service include access to
voice mail?

 Il y a des dérangements téléphoniques. *(eel ya day de-rahzh-mah tay-lay-fo-neek):* There are phone interruptions.

Nothing is more annoying than a phone call that is *interrompu* (interrupted) when you are trying to *prendre rendez-vous* (make an appointment or a date) or check on something important. Common disruptions are due to shortage of *crédits* (units) on your *Télécarte* or *carte SIM* or *un manque de réception* (lack of a signal) on your cell phone. The following phrases might prove useful if you experience problems with your phone.

**Je n'ai plus de crédits sur mon
portable.**
zheuh nay plU deuh kray-dee sUr
moh por-tabl

I have no units left on my cell phone.

Je n'ai pas de réception ici.
zheuh nay pa deuh re-sep-syoh
ee-see

I do not have a signal here.

Je viens de perdre le signal.
zheuh vyeh deuh per-dr leuh
see-nyal

I just lost the signal.

**Je rappellerai dans un petit
moment.**
zheuh ra-pel-ray dah zuh peuh-tee
mo-mah

I will call back in a moment.

Jusqu'à quelle heure le café est-il ouvert? *(zhUs-ka kel euhr leuh ka-fay ay-teel oo-ver):* Until what time is the café open?

This is where French people, young and old, come for coffee or a drink, to relax, to meet with friends, to watch passersby, and to take a break from work. In villages, cafés are especially wonderful places to watch the local scene, and they are often centrally located so you will be witness to many everyday activities. Most *cafés*, also called *cafés-bars*, are locally owned and run by the owner. Often the owners live right above their *café*.

Once you have found the local *café* you really like, check its business hours. A sign in front will say something like: *ouvert de 15 heures à 24 heures* (open from 3 P.M. to 12 A.M.). Some cafés are open for *le petit déjeuner* (breakfast), *le déjeuner* (lunch), and *le dîner* (dinner). Others are only open for certain shifts.

In some cafés items cost more when you are *assis* (seated) than *debout* (standing) at the bar. Every café displays *le menu* (an official price list) showing prices both at the bar and seated. Look for this list displayed near the entrance to the café.

You must order something when sitting at a table, but you do not need to order more than one item. No one minds how long you sit at a table inside or outside.

Some cafés turn into restaurants at lunchtime. If you see the waiters putting tablecloths on the outside tables, they are getting ready to serve lunch; it isn't a good idea to sit down at one of these tables unless you plan to have lunch.

Le café du bas est ouvert de 15 heures à 24 heures. leuh ka-fay dU ba ay too-ver deuh kih zeuhr a vih kat reuhr	The downstairs café is open from 3 P.M. to 12 A.M.

Vous connaissez un cybercafé pas trop cher? *(voo ko-nay-say uh see-ber-ka-fay pa tro sher):* Do you know a cybercafé that isn't too expensive?

French *cybercafés* have made a leap forward in convenience, but prices are often quite high (often eight to nine euros per hour). At a *cybercafé* you can *surfer/naviguer le web* (surf the Web) as well as *recevoir et envoyer des e-mails/mails* (receive and send e-mail). For *un supplément* (an extra charge), you can usually also use peripherals like *l'imprimante* (printer), *le scanner* (scanner), and *le graveur de CD* (CD-ROM burner). Some *cybercafés* have their own *sites web* (websites), which give details of access, opening hours, and activities. They will nearly always have cable or *ADSL* (DSL) Internet access. You probably already know that a number of Internet providers offer free e-mail accounts accessible from any computer connected to the Web.

Est-ce que vous connaissez un cybercafé sympa?
es-keuh voo kon-nes-say uh see-ber ka-fay sih-pa

Do you know a cool cybercafé?

Je voudrais une heure d'Internet.
zheuh voo-dray Un euhr dih-ter-net

I would like one hour of Internet.

Quel est le supplément pour l'imprimante?
kel ay leuh sU-play-mah poor lih-pree-maht

What is the surcharge for the printer?

Chapter 18

Sports

 Qui joue aujourd'hui? *(kee zhoo o-zhoor-dwee)*: Who's playing today?

Some of the most popular sports in France are *le basket-ball* and *le football*. Be aware that when the French talk about *le football*, they mean soccer. *Le football américain* is American-style football. France's national soccer team *Les Bleus* made the French proud by winning the World Cup in 1998 and the European Cup in 2000. Also very popular in France is *le rugby*; the first French rugby team dates back to 1872. To find out who is playing, ask anyone: *Qui joue aujourd'hui?*

C'est la Coupe du Monde.   It's the World Cup.

say la koop dU mohd

C'est le Tournoi des Nations.   It's the All-Nations' Tournament.

say leuh toor-nwa day na-syoh

Qui gagne? *(kee ga-nyeuh):* Who's winning?

Le cyclisme (cycling) is also very popular in France, with thousands of riders cycling every day as professionals, serious amateurs, and for pleasure. The *Tour de France* is one of the world's most watched spectator sports. Fans make predictions as to who has a chance to win various stages and the race itself: *Qui va gagner?* (Who's going to win?) Locals look forward to the racers coming through their town or village. If you want to know where the cyclists will be coming through today, ask: *Par où passent-ils aujourd'hui?*

The race lasts up to three weeks and is held every July. The route changes each year. *Le point de départ* (the starting point) varies and is often in one of France's neighboring countries. There are numerous *étapes* (stages); the winner of a stage gets to wear the *maillot jaune* (yellow jersey). The race always ends on the *Champs-Élysées* in Paris. From fans you will hear phrases such as *l'équipe* (the team), *le meilleur* (the best), *le plus d'endurance* (the most endurance), and *le favori* (the favorite).

Qui va gagner l'étape?	Who is going to win the stage?
kee va ga-nyay lay-tap	
Qui est le favori?	Who is the favorite?
kee ay leuh fa-vo-ree	
Quel est le vainqueur de l'étape?	Who is the winner of the stage?
kel ay leuh vih-keuhr deuh lay-tap	
Est-ce qu'il y a encore une chance?	Is there still a chance?
es keel ya ah-kor Un shahs	
Par où passent-ils?	Where are they coming through?
par oo pas-teel	

Où est le gym? *(oo ay leuh zheem):* Where is the gym?

While it is true that the French are not as eager to join a gym as their American counterparts, and many of them will tell you that they get plenty of exercise the "natural" way by doing lots of walking in the normal course of a day and by cycling on the weekend, there are nevertheless *des gyms* (gyms) where you can work on staying *en forme* (in shape). In addition, more and more French hotels have a *salle de sports* (exercise room) or a spa for their guests. At a large hotel, you can even sign up for a *session d'entraînement* (training session). You might, of course, meet many Americans at your class!

Quel est le tarif pour une session   What is the rate for a training session?
  d'entraînement?
kel ay leuh ta-reef poor Un ses-syoh
   dah-tren-mah

 Quel est le pronostic dans la première/deuxième course?
(kel ay leuh pro-nos-teek dah la preuh-myer/deuh-zhyem koors): What is the prediction for the first/second race?

France has many *courses hippiques* (horse races) and *hippodrome*s (racetracks). Many French enjoy watching horse racing. The *PMU,* or *Pari Mutuel Urbain,* is a French conglomerate created to promote and manage horse-race betting. The French government has given the *PMU* a monopoly over this activity. It allows people to bet on different types of races and according to different systems, such as: *le jeu simple*, a simple bet that consists of predicting who the winning horse will be, or *le tiercé,* which consists of betting on who the top three winners will be, in the correct order.

Les courts de tennis sont-ils disponibles? *(lay koor deuh tennis soh teel dees-po-nee-bl):* Are any tennis courts available?

For avid tennis players, it is easy to find a tennis court anywhere in France, where it is an amazingly popular sport. Tourists can usually get an *abonnement de courte durée* (temporary membership) *au club* (at the local club) for a nominal fee, or they can look for one of the many vacation sites (some in *châteaux*) that offer tennis facilities: *Des courts de tennis sont disponibles*. If you're in Paris during May and June, you can get tickets to *des matchs de qualité internationale* (some world-class games) at the famous Roland-Garros stadium, where you can see the French Open between mid-May and early June. You may also want to visit the new tennis museum, the *Tenniseum*. There you will learn that the *jeu de paume* (game of the palms, because it was originally played with the hands, before the invention of racquets) is the predecessor of tennis.

Pay attention to the different meanings of the French word *amateur. Être amateur de tennis* (etr a-ma-teuhr deuh ten-nees) means that you are into watching and playing tennis informally, whereas, *faire du tennis amateur* (fer dU ten-nees a-ma-teuhr) means to play serious amateur, nonprofessional tennis.

Je suis amateur de tennis.	I am always ready to play tennis./
zheuh swee a-ma-teuhr deuh	I love tennis.
ten-nees	
Je fais du tennis amateur.	I play nonprofessional tennis.
zheuh fay dU ten-nees a-ma-teuhr	
Je veux jouer au tennis tous	I want to play tennis every day.
les jours.	
zheuh veuh zhoo-ay o ten-nees	
too lay zhoor	

Allez-y! *(a-lay zee):* Go!

While watching your favorite team about to score, cheer the players on by shouting: *Allez-y!* (Go for it!) When you feel they should move forward, shout: *En avant!* After they make a goal, shout *À la bonne heure!* (Finally!) or *C'est ça!* (That's it!) to show your satisfaction. Shout *Bravo!* to congratulate them.

Allons-y!	Let's go!
a-loh zee	
En avant!	Forward!
a na-vah	
À la bonne heure!	Finally!
a la bon neuhr	
C'est ça!	That's it!
say sa	
Bravo!	Bravo!
bra-vo	

 Vive…! *(veev):* Long live . . . !

Enthusiastic soccer fans are often heard shouting out *Vive les Bleus!*, literally translated, "Long live the Blues!" *Les Bleus* refers to the players on the French national soccer team.

French presidents are known for ending their speeches to the nation with the phrase: *Vive la France! Vive les Français!* (Long live France! Long live the French!)

Charles de Gaulle, who served as the first president of the Fifth Republic, from 1959 to 1969, is remembered in Québec, Canada, for a speech in summer 1967 that included the Québec sovereignty slogan: *Vive le Québec libre!* (Long live free Québec!)

Chapter 19

Weather

 Que dit la météo? *(keuh dee la may-tay-o):* What's the weather forecast?

If you want to know what the weather will be like for the next few days, turn on the TV and watch *la météo* (the weather report) or *les prévisions météorologiques* (the weather forecast). Should you hear *On annonce des tempêtes de neige* (We forecast snowstorms), you might want to limit your outings. Should you hear *Il y a une canicule* (There's an intense heat wave), find *un endroit climatisé* (an air-conditioned place) (euh nah-drwa klee-ma-tee-zay) for the next few days.

On annonce de la pluie. o na-nohs deuh la plwee	They/We forecast rain.
On annonce des orages. o na-nohs day zo-razh	They/We forecast storms.
On annonce des tempêtes de neige. o na-nohs day tah-pet deuh nezh	They/We forecast snowstorms.

Il va y avoir une période
   de sécheresse.

eel va ee a-vwar Un pay-ryod deuh
   say-shres

There is going to be a drought.

Il y a une canicule.

eel ya Un ka-nee-kUl

We're having a heat wave.

 Quel temps va-t-il faire? *(kel tah va teel fer)*: What is the weather going to be like?

Whether you're in the city, near the beach, or in the mountains, you will want to know the weather before planning your day. Ask the locals; they are most likely to be reliable sources and be able to give you good advice.

Il va faire chaud.

eel va fer sho

It's going to be hot.

Il va faire froid.

eel va fer frwa

It's going to be cold.

Il fait frais aujourd'hui.

eel fay fray o-zhoor-dwee

It's cool today.

Préparez-vous à des orages.

pray-pa-ray voo a day zo-razh

Get ready for storms.

Il fait du brouillard ce matin.

eel fay dU broo-yar seuh ma-tih

It's foggy this morning.

Prenez un parapluie!

preuh-nay uh pa-ra-plwee

Take an umbrella!

Il va certainement neiger.

eel va ser-ten-mah ne-zhay

It's certainly going to snow.

Quelle est la température? *(kel ay la tah-pay-ra-tUr):*
What's the temperature?

In France, temperatures are measured in centigrade (Celsius) degrees. In the Celsius system, 0 degrees (°) Celsius is the melting point of ice. The boiling point of water is 100° Celsius. In the Fahrenheit scale, used primarily in the United States, the freezing point of water is 32° and the boiling point is 212°. It may make it easier for you to understand the weather if you convert the Celsius temperature to Fahrenheit. When you read a temperature in Celsius degrees, convert it to the Fahrenheit system by multiplying the temperature in Celsius by $\frac{9}{5}$ and adding 32 to the result.

For example, if you want to know the Fahrenheit equivalent of 26° C, do the following:

$$26 \times \tfrac{9}{5} = 47$$
$$47 + 32 = 79° F$$

Or simply ask someone at your hotel what the weather will be like. You can expect answers such as the following:

Il fait vingt-six degrés.	It is twenty-six degrees (Celsius).
Il va faire dix-neuf degrés.	It is going to be nineteen degrees (Celsius).

Il fait un froid de canard. *(eel fay uh frwa deuh ka-nar):*
It is very cold.

This is an expression used to describe a cold spell. It is a reference to the cold weather typical of the *canard* (duck) hunting season.

Some other phrases about weather refer to dogs. To say that the weather is really bad, you will hear people say either *Il fait un temps de chien* (This weather is fitting only for dogs), or a somewhat animal-friendlier phrase *Il fait un temps à ne pas mettre un chien dehors.* (It's the kind of weather where you don't put a dog out.)

Il fait un temps de chien.   The weather is really bad.

eel fay uh tah deuh shyeh

Il fait un temps à ne pas mettre   The weather is really bad.
   un chien dehors.

eel fay uh tah a neuh pa metr uh

   shyeh deuh-or

 Il pleut des cordes. *(eel pleuh day kord):* It is pouring rain.

There are many phrases about the weather that appeal to the visual senses, such as: *Il pleut des cordes.* The literal meaning of this phrase is: It is raining ropes. The suggestive visual power of the ropes emphasizes the thickness of the downpour. Similarly, the phrases *le brouillard est épais* (the fog is thick), *le soleil luit* (the sun is shining), and *la brume se lève* (the mist is lifting) are visual images.

Other weather expressions such as *le vent souffle* (the wind is blowing), *le tonnerre gronde* (the thunder is roaring) trigger our auditory sense.

Le brouillard est épais.   The fog is thick.

leuh broo-yar ay tay-pay

La brume se lève.   The mist is lifting.

la brUm seuh lev

Le soleil luit.   The sun is shining.

leuh so-lay lwee

Le vent souffle.   The wind is blowing.

leuh vah soo-fl

Le tonnerre gronde.   The thunder is roaring.
leuh ton-ner grohd

 Je meurs de chaleur. *(zheuh meuhr deuh sha-leuhr)*: I am dying of the heat.

If you want to dramatize and emphasize how hot you are, instead of saying: *J'ai chaud* (I feel hot), say: *Je meurs de chaleur* (I am dying of the heat). If you're sweating and need cool air, say: *Je transpire. Il me faut de l'air frais.*

J'ai chaud.   I'm hot.
zhay sho
Je transpire.   I'm sweating.
zheuh trahs-peer
Il me faut de l'air frais.   I need fresh air.
eel meuh fo deuh ler fray

 Je grelotte de froid. *(zheuh greuh-lot deuh frwa)*: I'm shivering from cold.

Similarly, if you want to stress how cold you are, instead of saying *J'ai froid*, say: *Je grelotte de froid* (I am shivering from cold), or more emphatically, say: *Je claque des dents!* (My teeth are chattering!)

J'ai froid.   I am cold.
zhay frwa
Je claque des dents!   My teeth are chattering!
zheuh klak day dah

Chapter 20

Conversational Phrases

 Je suis ravi(e) d'accepter. *(zheuh swee ra-vee dak-sep-tay):* I am delighted to accept.

If someone says to you *Je vous invite à passer une semaine chez moi à Cannes. D'accord?* (zheuh voo zih-veet a pa-say Un seuh-men shay mwa a kan da-kor) (I'm inviting you to spend a week at my house in Cannes. OK?), quickly answer: *Je suis ravi(e) d'accepter, merci!* (I am delighted to accept, thank you!) or: *Je me réjouis de pouvoir vous rendre visite!* (I am delighted/I am excited to be able to visit you!) An invitation to dine at *un restaurant à trois étoiles* (a three-star restaurant) might elicit an even stronger reaction of delight such as: *Je suis aux anges!* (I'm in heaven!)

Now imagine someone asks you how you feel about a happy event such as your friend's upcoming wedding. Answer that you are happy about it by saying: *J'en suis heureux/heureuse.* (I'm happy about it.) You would choose this phrase to express a deep level of happiness. If you are pleased about something less important, perhaps a small gift you received, use the phrase: *J'en suis content/contente.* (I'm pleased with it.)

Je me réjouis de pouvoir vous rendre visite.	I am delighted to be able to visit you.
zheuh meuh ray-zhwee deuh poo-vwar voo rah-dr vee-zeet	
Je suis aux anges!	I'm in heaven!
zheuh swee o zahzh	
J'en suis heureux/heureuse.	I'm happy about it.
zhah swee zeuh-reuh/zeuh-reuhz	
J'en suis content/contente.	I'm pleased about it.
zhah swee koh-tah/koh-taht	

Quel plaisir! *(kel play-zeer):* What a pleasure!

This phrase is often used when people see each other again after a significant separation: *Quel plaisir de vous/de te revoir!* (kel play-zeer deuh voo/deuh teuh reuh-vwar) (What a pleasure to see you again!) The meaning of the word *plaisir* is best understood by going back to its root and remembering that the verb *plaire*, from which the noun *plaisir* is derived, means "to please." By contrast, use the phrase *Quel bonheur!* to express your pleasure when the feeling is much deeper, for example, as in saying: *Quel bonheur d'être amoureux!* (kel bo-neuhr detr a-moo-reuh) (What happiness it is to be in love!) If you want to express what joy it is to spend precious time with your friends, say: *Quelle joie de passer ces moments avec vous!* (kel zhwa deuh pa-say say mo-mah a-vek voo)

Quel bonheur!	What happiness!
kel bo-neuhr	
Quelle joie!	What joy!
kel zhwa	

Je suis fou/folle de joie! *(zheuh swee foo/fol deuh zhwa):* I am mad with joy!

The phrase *Je suis fou/folle de joie* (I am mad with joy) or *Je meurs de joie* (I'm just dying of joy) are to be used in moments of intense and delirious happiness. Say you heard that you won *la loterie* (the lottery). After all, it isn't every day that one goes mad or dies from happiness. While waiting to receive your *prix de la loterie*, you might well say *Je suis fou/folle d'impatience* (I am mad with impatience), or *Je délire* (zheuh day-leer) (I am delirious), or even *Je meurs d'impatience de recevoir mon prix* (zheuh meuhr dih-pa-syahs deuh reuh-seuh-vwar moh pree) (literally, I am dying of impatience/I can't wait to receive my prize). In French, any strong emotion can seemingly drive you crazy, delirious, or even kill you.

Je meurs de joie.	I'm mad with joy.
zheuh meuhr deuh zhwa	
Je meurs d'impatience.	I'm dying with impatience.
zheuh meuhr dih-pa-syahs	
Je suis fou/folle d'impatience.	I'm mad with impatience.
zheuh swee foo/fol dih-pa-syahs	
Je délire.	I'm delirious.
zheuh day-leer	

 C'est super! *(say sU-per):* That's super!

Are you amazed at what a good seat you got at the theater? Exclaim *C'est super. Quelle bonne place!* (That's super. What a good seat!) Are you impressed at how well your friend speaks French? Then exclaim: *C'est épatant comme tu parles bien le français!* (say tay-pa-tah kom tU parl byeh leuh frah-say) (It's amazing how well you speak French!)

Watching the Paris cityscape from the top of the *Tour Eiffel* (Eiffel Tower) on a clear day, you will surely get excited and exclaim: *C'est fantastique, cette vue!* (say fah-tas-teek set vU) (This view is fantastic!) Did you just receive exciting news, such as an invitation to spend a few weeks in Paris? Exclaim: *C'est formidable. J'arrive!* (say for-mee-da-bl zha-reev) (Fantastic. I'm on my way!)

C'est épatant!	Amazing!
say tay-pa-tah	
C'est magnifique!	Magnificent!
say ma-nyee-feek	
C'est fantastique!	Fantastic!
say fah-tas-teek	
C'est formidable!	Terrific!
say for-mee-da-bl	

 Tant mieux! *(tah myeuh):* So much the better!/All the better!

Did you just find out that the weather will be great all week during your trip? You can use any of the previously mentioned phrases to show your pleasure, or you can moderate your response by saying *Tant mieux!* (So much the better!) If you find out your friend arrived on time at his destination despite a late departure, tell him/her *Tant mieux pour toi!* This is the equivalent of: I'm happy for you.

Les trains français sont ponctuels.	French trains are on time. So much
Tant mieux!	the better!
lay trih frah-say soh pohk-tU-el	
tah myeuh	

Le tour guidé est en anglais.	The guided tour is in English. So
Tant mieux!	much the better!
leuh toor gee-day ay tah nah-glay	
tah myeuh	

 Zut! *(zUt)*: Darn!

This is a harmless exclamation which can be used in just about any situation where you are disappointed, taken aback, or even surprised. Use it when you realize that you are late to an appointment, if you just dropped something, or if your team is not playing up to your expectations. It serves almost every purpose. If you want to emphasize your emotion or reaction, simply add the word *alors*, and say *Zut alors!* As often in French, for a much stronger effect, repeat the word, saying: *Zut de zut de zut!* People around you will know that you really mean it! However, as a nonnative, please do not use *Merde* or *Merde alors* without checking very carefully what company you're in: it's OK perhaps to use among your very closest pals, but NEVER resort to it in a business setting, with older people, or with new acquaintances. Note, however, that it's quite commonly used by the French; it is the equivalent of "sh—."

Zut alors!	Darn it!
zU ta-lor	
Zut de zut de zut!	Darn it!
zUt deuh zUt deuh zUt	

Ah non, quand même! *(a noh kah mem):* No way!

You might say or hear this if another driver cuts you off or cuts your cab driver off, for example. The phrase expresses both surprise and anger. The phrase *Il ne faut pas exagérer!/Faut pas exagérer!* is used similarly; it means "Don't exaggerate" (not often used in English). A somewhat more emphatic outcry would be: *Non de non de non* (noh deuh noh deuh noh). The combination of repetition and alliteration within the phrase makes it much more powerful, as in the previously mentioned *Zut de zut de zut!*

Non de non de non!   Absolutely not!
noh deuh noh deuh noh
Il ne faut pas exagérer!/Faut   Let's not exaggerate!
   pas exagérer!
eel neuh fo pa zeg-za-zhay-ray/fo
   pa zeg-za-zhay-ray

 Ne m'en parlez pas! *(neuh mah par-lay pa):* Don't even mention it!

In spite of its negative tone, this phrase can be used in reaction to a comment that you totally agree with, especially when the original comment has a negative slant. For example, if someone just said: *Il fait un temps de chien* (This is horrible weather, not even good enough for dogs), and you agree, say: *Ne m'en parlez pas*, to show how displeased you are yourself with the weather.

On the other hand, one uses the phrase *N'en parlons pas* if someone broaches a topic you really do not want to consider. For example, if someone mentions politics and you do not care to get into it, quickly state: *N'en parlons pas, s'il vous/te plaît.* (Let's not discuss this, please.)

However, the phrase *Je ne veux pas en entendre parler* (I don't want to hear about it) can sound abrasive; it shows great displeasure or anger at the very mention of a topic.

Ne m'en parlez pas!	Don't talk about it!/Don't even
neuh mah par-lay pa	mention it!
N'en parlons pas!	Let's not talk about it!
nah par-loh pa	
Je ne veux pas en entendre parler.	I don't want to hear about it.
zheuh neuh veuh pa za nah-tah-dr	
par-lay	

 Jamais de la vie! *(zha-may deuh la vee):* Not on your life!

Use this phrase to object strongly to anything that you feel strongly about. If someone dares to imply that you might try smoking, and you are vehemently opposed to it, say *Jamais de la vie!* (Not on your life!) Or you might use another phrase stating something completely impossible such as *quand les poules auront des dents* ([I'll start smoking] when chickens grow teeth [in other words, never]).

Quand les poules auront	When chickens grow teeth.
des dents.	
kah lay pool o-roh day dah	

J'en ai assez de ce vacarme! *(zha nay a-say deuh seuh va-karm)*: I've had enough of that noise!

If something really gets on your nerves, for example, the loud music the children are playing, you might be justified in saying *Ça me suffit, ce bruit*, or *J'en ai assez de ce vacarme* (both mean: "I've had enough of that noise."). Someone less polite or less formal might say *J'en ai marre!* or *J'en ai ras le bol!* (I'm sick of it/of that!) These exclamations have the same meaning, but are used more generally (not just for noise) and are rather more familiar.

J'en ai marre!	I've had enough (of it)!
zha nay mar	
J'en ai ras le bol!	I'have had enough (of it)!
zha nay ral bol	
Ça me suffit, ce bruit!	I've had enough of this noise!
sa meuh sU-fee seuh brwee	
Ça me tape sur les nerfs.	It/That gets on my nerves.
sa meuh tap sUr lay nerf	

 Ça ne vaut pas la peine. *(sa neuh vo pa la pen)*: It's not worth it.

If you tried several times, say, to find a less expensive plane ticket to some destination, and it was in vain, you may just throw in the towel, and say: *Ça ne vaut pas la peine, je ne le trouverai pas.* (sa neuh vo pa la pen zheuh neuh leuh troo-vray pa) (It's not worth it. I won't find it.) When a friend urges you to try again, you will probably repeat yourself, or say: *Vraiment, ça ne vaut pas le coup!* (vray-mah sa neuh vo pa leuh koo) (It's really not worth it!) You'll sound even more pessimistic when you say: *Ça ne sert à rien.* (It's useless.)

Let's say you were told to try getting your plane ticket through a travel agency, and this does not work for you either, you exclaim: *Ça ne rime à rien de téléphoner à l'agence: aucun résultat!* (sa neuh reem a ryeh deuh tay-lay-fo-nay a la-zhahs o-kuh ray-zUl-ta) (It's worthless calling the agency: no result!)

À quoi bon?	What's the point?
a kwa boh	
Ça ne vaut pas le coup.	It's not worth it.
sa neuh vo pa leuh koo	
Ça ne sert à rien.	It's useless.
sa neuh ser ta ryeh	
Ça ne rime à rien.	It is to no avail.
sa neuh reem a ryeh	

 Ça n'a pas d'importance. *(sa na pa dih-por-tahs):* It doesn't matter.

The waiter just asked you what type of mineral water you prefer: *Quelle eau minérale préférez-vous?* (kel o mee-nay-ral pray-fay-ray voo). If the brand doesn't matter to you, say: *Ça n'a pas d'importance.* You can also use these synonyms: *Ça n'a aucune importance* (sa na o-kUn ih-por-tahs) or *Peu importe* (peuh ih-port).

Now imagine that you have been looking forward to a concert, and the only seats available are in the back of the hall. If you still want to go and don't really care that the seats are not the best, say: *Ça m'est égal. Je veux assister à ce concert.* (sa may tay-gal zheuh veuh a-sees-tay a seuh koh-ser) (I don't care. I want to attend this concert.) Now you're waiting in line to get into the concert hall, and the people in front of you brag about the great seats they have. You can *être beau joueur* (be a good sport) and exclaim *Tant mieux pour vous!* (tah myeuh poor voo) (Good for you!), or you can act aloof and say: *Ça ne me fait ni chaud ni froid.* (sa neuh meuh fay nee sho nee frwa) (It doesn't matter to me./It leaves me cold/indifferent.)

Ça n'a aucune importance.	It doesn't matter at all.
sa na o-kUn ih-por-tahs	
Peu importe.	It is of little importance.
peuh ih-port	
Ça m'est égal.	I don't care.
sa may tay-gal	
Ça ne me fait ni chaud ni froid.	It does not affect me at all.
sa neuh meuh fay nee sho nee frwa	

 Plus ça change plus c'est la même chose. *(plU sa shahzh plU say la mem shoz):* The more things change the more they stay the same.

If you want to express disappointment that transportation in France is still disturbed by frequent strikes (you'd expected it to change under President Sarkozy), use this old saying: *Plus ça change, plus c'est la même chose.*

You reserved *une voiture de location avec climatisation* (a rental car with air conditioning), but when you arrive to pick it up, you're told that there are none available. To compensate, the agency offers you *un surclassement* (uh sUr-klas-mah) (an upgrade), but still without air conditioning. This won't really change your situation, so you say *Ça ne change rien.* (sa neuh shahzh ryeh) (That doesn't change anything.)

When you check into your hotel, you notice that your room faces *une rue bruyante* (a busy/noisy street). You ask for another room, but the new one is still noisy because it is poolside. You are right to exclaim: *Mais ça revient au même!* (may sa reuh-vyeh o mem) (But that amounts to the same thing!)

Ça ne change rien!   It doesn't change anything!
sa neuh shahzh ryeh

Mais ça revient au même.   It amounts to the same thing.
may sa reuh-vyeh o mem

 Après moi, le déluge! *(a-pray mwa leuh day-lUzh)*: After me, the deluge!

This is a famous line attributed to King Louis XV (1710–1774) toward the end of his life. Like his predecessor (and great-grandfather) Louis XIV, the Sun King, Louis XV lived in luxury as his subjects descended into greater and greater poverty. The saying *Après moi, le déluge!* (After me, come the floods!) epitomizes the egocentrism that shows a total lack of concern about what will happen after one's own life is over. Even though the expression is based on eighteenth-century events, it has become an everyday phrase used by people to proclaim (often ironically) that they don't care about what happens as long as they get what they want.

 À chacun son goût! *(a sha-kuh soh goo)*: To each his own!

You could use this phrase if you find someone's taste in clothing or food surprising or even shocking. You can say *à chacun son goût* (to each his own) in a *laissez-vivre* (les-say vee-vr) (let live) way or in a disapproving, sarcastic way. Your tone of voice, your body language, and the context will confirm what you mean.

C'est la vie! *(say la vee):* That's life!

This fatalistic statement often points out a reality check or a moment when one gives up hope of being able to change a situation, without falling into despair or blaming anyone in particular for the disappointment. If you can't get the room, the rental car, the concert seats you wanted, but you're determined not to let it ruin your vacation, say: *C'est la vie!* and move on.

 Bâtir des châteaux en Espagne. *(ba-teer day sha-to a nes-pa-nyeuh):* To imagine or dream about unreachable things.

If someone tells you *Tu bâtis des châteaux en Espagne* (You're building castles in Spain), you have been labeled a dreamer, and, to your friend, your dream seems too far-fetched to come true. This very old expression may have its source in medieval times when *les Maures* (the Moors) were constantly invading Spain but were unable to establish themselves there for lack of defensive structures like *châteaux* (castles). The phrase thus came to symbolize the impossibility of an endeavor.

Similarly, a project that seems overly romantic or idealistic can be labeled *un projet chimérique* (uh pro-zhay shee-may-reek). In English, the closest translation for *chimérique* is "quixotic," after the legendary Spaniard Don Quixote, who battled windmills in his romantic efforts to prove his righteousness and courage. Have you known idealistic people who think they can change the world? There are those who support such idealism and others who think it's all fancy and fantasy. The latter type is likely to make this comment: *C'est un projet chimèrique. Laisse tomber!* (It's a fanciful project. Drop it!)

Other remarks that *les pessimistes* (pessimists) or *les réalistes* (real-ists) will make in the face of idealistic enterprises are: *Reviens sur terre* (Come back to earth) or *Tu rêves* (You're dreaming).

Laisse tomber.	Drop it.
les toh-bay	
Oublie tout ça.	Forget all that.
oo-blee too sa	
Reviens sur terre.	Come back to earth.
reuh-vyeh sUr ter	
Tu rêves.	You're dreaming.
tU rev	

 C'est une promesse. *(say tUn pro-mes)*: That's a promise.

On *ira au cinema samedi; c'est une promesse* (o nee-ra o see-nay-ma sam-dee say tUn pro-mes) (We'll go to the movies on Saturday; that's a promise) is a sentence mom and dad might make to their children.

Je ne mentirai plus jamais; c'est juré (zheuh neuh mah-tee-ray plU zha-may say zhU-ray) (I will never tell a lie again; I swear) is a promise a child might make to his parents. Or a child accused of some mischief might deny it by saying: *Je ne l'ai pas fait; je te le jure.* (zheuh neuh lay pa fay; zheuh teuh leuh zhUr) (I swear I didn't do it.)

If you don't have the time to continue a phone conversation, say: *Je te promets de te rappeler demain.* (zheuh teuh pro-may deuh teuh rap-lay deuh-mih) (I promise to call you back tomorrow.) Do you want to further reassure your interlocutor? You can add: *Je t'assure/Crois-moi, on parlera demain.* (zheuh ta-sUr/krwa mwa oh par-leuh-ra deuh-mih) (I assure you/Believe me, we'll talk tomorrow.)

C'est juré.	I swear./It's an oath.
say zhU-ray	
Je te le jure.	I swear to you.
zheuh teuh leuh zhUr	
Je promets de te rappeler demain.	I promise to call you back tomorrow.
zheuh pro-may deuh teuh rap-lay	
deuh-mih	
Je t'assure.	I assure you.
zheuh ta-sUr	
Crois-moi, on parlera demain!	Believe me, we'll talk tomorrow!
krwa mwa oh par-leuh-ra deuh-mih	

 Tout à fait! *(too ta fay):* Yes, of course!

This is a very common response to a question and is frequently used instead of *Oui*. Someone asks you if you received an invitation, say: *Tout à fait!* to express that you did. Answer: *Mais tout à fait!* and you are really asserting that you did.

Less fashionable, but just as correct, is the phrase *Bien sûr* (Of course) or the more forceful *Mais bien sûr* which suggests: How could you doubt it?

As a response to a negative question, such as: *Vous ne venez pas ce soir?* (voo neuh veuh-nay pa seuh swar) (Aren't you coming tonight?), use the phrase *Mais si!* (Yes, certainly I am!) The word *si*, used to say "yes" in French, contradicts the negative suggestion (that you might not come) in the original question.

Mais tout à fait!	Absolutely!
may too ta fay	

Mais bien sûr!   Yes, of course!

may byeh sUr

Mais si.   Yes.

may see

 D'accord. *(da-kor):* OK.

The French use the English utterance "OK" routinely, but the French expression *D'accord* is just as common: *Tu veux sortir dîner? —D'accord.* (Do you want to go out to dinner? —OK.); *Ce concert est vraiment super, non? —Je suis d'accord.* (This concert is really great, don't you think? —I agree.) On the other hand, if you want to acknowledge that your interlocutor is correct, use the phrase *avoir raison* (a-vwar ray-zoh) as in this example: *Ce genre de tailleur n'est plus à la mode. —Vous avez raison.* (This kind of suit is no longer in style. —You're right.)

Tu veux sortir dîner? —D'accord.   Do you want to go out to dinner?

tU veuh sor-teer dee-nay da-kor   —OK.

Ce concert est vraiment super,   This concert is really great, don't

non? —Je suis d'accord.   you think? —I agree.

seuh koh-ser ay vray-mah sUper

   noh zheuh swee da-kor

Ce genre de tailleur n'est plus   This type of suit is no longer in

à la mode. —Vous avez raison.   style. —You're right.

seuh zhahr deuh ta-yeuhr nay plU

   a la mod voo za-vay ray-zoh

Joyeux anniversaire! *(zwa-yeuh za-nee-ver-ser):* Happy birthday!

Use the phrase *Joyeux anniversaire* to wish someone a happy birthday. If you cannot attend a *fête d'anniversaire* (birthday party) you've been invited to, send a *cadeau* (gift) or a *carte de vœux* (greeting card). If you can attend the celebration, you will likely be treated to a delicious *gâteau d'anniversaire* decorated with the name of the birthday person and the appropriate number of *bougies* (candles).

Christmas celebrations vary throughout France, but Santa Claus is known as Père *Noël,* and he is sometimes accompanied by Père Fouettard (Father Whip) who keeps track of who has been good or bad. Children open their gifts on Christmas Eve or Christmas Day, but parents and other adults must wait until *le Nouvel An* (New Year's Day) for their gifts. Tradition demands that *le Réveillon* (Christmas dinner) be served at midnight on December 24. A special Christmas cake, *la bûche de Noël* (Yule log), is served as dessert. The *Réveillon* meal varies from region to region. For example, in Paris, it features raw oysters and *pâté de foie gras.* In Alsace, roast goose is served; in Burgundy, turkey with chestnuts; and in Brittany, *crêpes* (buckwheat pancakes) with sour cream.

Joyeux Noël!	Merry Christmas!
zhwa-yeuh no-el	
Joyeuse Hanoukka!	Happy Hanukkah!
zhwa-yeuhz a-noo-ka	
Bonne fête de Ramadan!	Best wishes for Ramadan!
bon fet deuh ra-ma-dah	

Bonne Année!	Happy New Year!
bo na-nay	
Bonne et Heureuse Année!	Happy New Year!
bon ay euh-reuhz a-nay	

 Meilleurs vœux! *(may-euhr veuh):* Best wishes!

On New Year's cards, you will read *Meilleurs vœux* or *Meilleurs souhaits* (Best wishes).

A get-well card will probably bear the phrase *Bonne convalescence* (Get well) or *Meilleurs souhaits pour une bonne convalescence* (Best wishes for a good convalescence).

Meilleurs souhaits!	Best wishes!
may-euhr soo-ay	
Bonne convalescence!	Get well!
bon koh-va-les-sahs	